# THE GREAT INFLATION

## A Monetarist View

BY HAROLD VAN B. CLEVELAND
AND W.H. BRUCE BRITTAIN

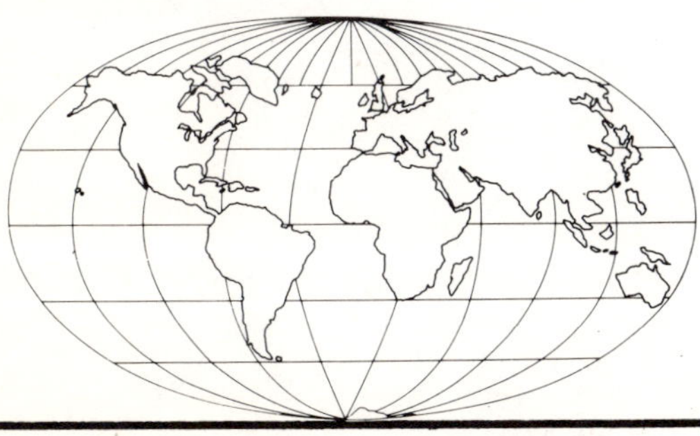

NPA Committee on
Changing International Realities

THE GREAT INFLATION:
A Monetarist View

CIR Report No. 1
NPA Report No. 148

Price $3.50

Library of Congress
Catalog Card Number 76-41068


A voluntary association incorporated under the laws of
the District of Columbia
1606 New Hampshire Avenue, N.W.
Washington, D.C. 20009

C 439

# Contents

## The Great Inflation: A Monetarist View

by Harold van B. Cleveland
and W.H. Bruce Brittain

# A Statement by the Committee on Changing International Realities

In the last few years, it has become increasingly evident that major economic and political changes have been taking place in the international system as a whole and in the position of the United States within it. These changes and others likely to occur—perhaps sooner than we expect—have important implications for U.S. policies, not only at the governmental level, but also for private business, labor unions, agricultural interests, and consumers. The Committee on Changing International Realities was formed in 1975 with representative leaders from the main functional groups in the private sector so as to help interpret the changing realities of the international system and contribute toward the formation of U.S. policies.

One of the most important new realities to emerge in the past few years was an unprecedented worldwide inflation of prices. The pervasive inflation that was generated during the first half of the 1970s was an important new development and as such is deserving of careful analysis. An indication of the novelty and importance of this event is the fact that it is already being referred to as the Great Inflation of the 1970s. Like the Great Depression of the 1930s, the Great Inflation of the 1970s is a highly complex phenomenon and a manifestation of worldwide interdependence, as no nation has escaped its impact. A variety of explanations are being offered of its origins, spread and future development, but it remains to be seen whether there will ever be a single generally accepted comprehensive account.

The authors of this study, Harold van B. Cleveland, advisor to the Committee on Changing International Realities, and W.H. Bruce Brittain, utilize one particular framework, the monetarist approach, to explain the causes of the Great Inflation. Their study illuminates part of a highly complex phenomenon and on this basis is deserving of the widest possible circulation. The Committee on Changing International Realities is therefore pleased to recommend that this study be published as a report signed by the authors. Without concurring in all of the specific analyses and conclusions advanced, the Committee recognizes the report as a contribution toward understanding the Great Inflation of the 1970s.

### Footnotes to the Statement

*In this interesting paper, the authors find a single, unifying explanation for the inflation of the past decade. They attempt to show that (1) the world money supply drives world inflation and (2) the U.S. money supply drives the world money supply, with some qualifications to the second proposition since exchange rates have become more flexible. It is a bold exercise, and an illuminating one. Any explanation of the recent inflation must give these factors important weight. But, we believe the authors drive their explanation too hard, requiring it to do too much. The analysis has several weaknesses and, as a result, the (largely implicit) policy recommendations are too simplistic.*

*First, if the money supply is as central as the authors suggest, we must ask what determines the money supply. The authors accuse nonmonetary theorists of inflation of regarding money creation as totally passive; they commit the opposite error of regarding it as totally unconstrained. In fact, national monetary authorities are not outside the economic and political system; they are part of it. When wages or prices rise for some independent reason, the monetary authorities are confronted with an immediate dilemma: to accommodate the rise and risk inflation, or not to accommodate it and risk unemployment. The authors admit as much in their advocacy of gradualism, but they fail to discuss the mechanism whereby gradualism avoids the dilemma.*

*Second, as their own data show, much credit expansion in other major countries was not due to reserve accruals of dollars, that is, was not due to balance-of-payments deficits of the United States. This point would have been even clearer if they had examined a longer list of countries: inflation occurred around the world, even in countries that did not have payments surpluses and even in countries that altered their exchange rates frequently. Even four of the six major countries examined by Cleveland and Brittain changed their exchange rates between 1967 and 1970, permitting or reflecting divergence of monetary conditions between these countries. Monetary linkage to the United States was present, but it was hardly lock-step.*

*Third, even within the monetarist approach espoused by the authors, the money supply is not the only determinant of prices. The important relationship is between demand for money and supply of money, as the authors recognize in some contexts. If world output and income fall, as they did when world grain production fell in 1972–73, or when the OPEC countries restricted the output of oil in order to raise prices in 1973–74, the price* level *will rise even without new monetary injections. The authors pay insufficient attention to those events, even within their own framework.*

*Fourth, an observation on method: in the face of admitted substantial differences in monetary growth (relative to real output) among nations, the authors argue we must look at price movements. In the face of admitted substantial differences in price performance (especially as regards Japan), the authors say we have to adjust for exchange-rate changes and allow for "measurement errors." How do we know there are measurement errors? Because the monetary theory espoused by the authors tells us monetary conditions must be the same among countries. In short, the theory is imposed upon the data rather than being supported by them; without independent evidence of measurement errors, the empirical argument is circular.*

*These observations are not meant to deny that unwise monetary policy played an important role in recent world inflation, or that the United States in the late 1960s was an important source of world inflation. Both are true. But, the authors' search for a single, sovereign explanation of recent inflation succeeds in illuminating only one corner of a much more complex phenomenon. Despite the authors' dutiful caveats, the main thrust of their account, by denying the significance of other factors, particularly on the supply side, risks misleading the reader and creating unwarranted complacency about our knowledge of what causes–and therefore what can cure–worldwide inflation.*–**Richard N. Cooper, Lawrence Krause and Marina v. N. Whitman**

*I share many of the views of the distinguished authors of* The Great Inflation. *From their study emerges a conclusion which is insufficiently clarified by the authors themselves. On page 53 they write, "But, as long as the world remains on a dollar standard, only the United States has it within its power to safeguard—or undermine—the general stability of the system as a whole." That is to say, only U.S. financial* self-discipline, *in the present floating exchange-rate regime, based on the reserve currency status of the dollar, can yield global price stability.*

*I should like to argue that if American leadership intends to submit* voluntarily *to such self-denying ordinances, the same leadership might reasonably ask the leading trading nations of the world to embody in a monetary agreement those same ordinances. Such a treaty should define a simple and efficacious monetary rule. Such a treaty would rule out official reserve currencies, and thereby eliminate the burdens and privileges of the reserve currency system based on the dollar. As the authors themselves suggest on pages 49 through 50, history has yielded enduring and stable exchange-rate regimes only when they have been based on fixed currency exchange rates and universal gold convertibility; and only when such a regime is upheld by the indisputable equilibrium leader—in the coming era, that is, by the United States.*

*The very operating principle of such a fixed exchange-rate regime, based on convertibility, would rule out the inflationary excesses sometimes caused by past monetary policies in the* reserve currency centers, *best exemplified by sterling in the 1920s and the dollar in the late 1960s and early 1970s. If the behavior of great nations, as of men, is to be governed by rules rather than by momentary impulses of self-interested politicians, the equilibrium leader itself, the United States, must elaborate a stable and lasting exchange-rate rule in a monetary treaty, a treaty which will have the force of law among the free nations of the world. Such a treaty will determine equitable fixed exchange-rate relationships based on gold convertibility. This treaty, developed under U.S. leadership, will bring to an end the age of inflation through which we are now living.*–**Lewis E. Lehrman**

*Bankers and capable economists, like the authors of this paper, along with money cranks and goldbugs, often have tried to explain economic phenomena by money alone. The Greenbacker inflationists were not different from the "sound money" men in this fascination with money and credit. This document is an excellent study of the monetary factors in the Great Inflation, and the authors carefully disclaim more for it. But, even such a well-guarded report tends to lead to over-simplified policy recommendations, the ignoring of monopoly in business and labor and the dismissing of government action of a "sociological" nature as a tool for fighting inflation.*–**Lauren K. Soth**

## Members of the Committee on Changing International Realities Signing the Statement

G. A. COSTANZO
*Chairman;* Vice Chairman, Citibank

HOWARD C. KAUFFMANN
*Chairman of the Executive Committee;* President, Exxon Corporation

JOHN MILLER
*Secretary of the Committee;* President, National Planning Association

JOSEPH H. ALLEN
Senior Vice President, United Technologies Corporation

WILLIAM S. ANDERSON
Chairman and President, NCR Corporation

ROBERT N. BEE
Senior Vice President, Wells Fargo Bank

HOWARD W. BELL
Director and Financial Vice President, Standard Oil Company of California

RICHARD M. BISSELL, JR.
Consultant, The Exchange

HARRY D. BROOKBY
Executive Vice President, Corporate Planning and Budgeting, Phillips Petroleum Company

ROBERT G. BROWN
Executive Vice President, Corporate Development, Eaton Corporation

CARLOS M. CANAL, JR.
Executive Vice President, Bankers Trust Company

J. G. CLARKE
Senior Vice President, Exxon Corporation

HARRY CONOVER
Vice President, Citibank

*RICHARD N. COOPER
Professor of International Economics, Yale University

JAMES E. CRAWFORD, JR.
Managing Director, A Group Vice President, Monsanto Company

W. C. DRUEHL
President, Del Monte International, Inc.

MURRAY H. FINLEY
General President, Amalgamated Clothing Workers of America

RAYMOND G. FISHER
Vice Chairman of the Board, Continental Can Company, Inc.

CHARLES S. GANOE
Senior Executive Vice President, The Fidelity Bank

J. PETER GRACE
President, W. R. Grace & Co.

ROGER W. GRAY
Professor, Food Research Institute, Stanford University

JAMES R. GREENE
Senior Vice President and Deputy General Manager, International Division, Manufacturers Hanover Trust Company

JOHN M. HENNESSY
Senior Vice President & Director, The First Boston Corporation

JOHN H. JACKSON
Professor of Law, The University of Michigan Law School

JEROME JACOBSON
Senior Vice President, The Bendix Corporation

G. GRIFFITH JOHNSON
Executive Vice President, Motion Picture Association of America, Inc.

MAYNARD W. JOHNSON
Regional Vice President, East Allis-Chalmers Corporation

*See footnotes to the Statement.

TOM KILLEFER
President, United States Trust Company of New York

*LAWRENCE B. KRAUSE
Senior Fellow, The Brookings Institution

BERNARD LARNER
Vice President, Lummus Company

JAMES E. LEE
President, Gulf Oil Corporation

*LEWIS E. LEHRMAN
President, Rite Aid Corporation

EDWARD LITTLEJOHN
Vice President, Public Affairs, Pfizer, Incorporated

WILLIAM J. McDONOUGH
Executive Vice President, The First National Bank of Chicago

WILLIAM R. MILLER
Senior Vice President, Bristol Myers Company; President, Bristol-Myers Company, International Division

ALFRED F. MIOSSI
Executive Vice President, Continental Illinois National Bank & Trust Company of Chicago

W. B. NICHOLSON
Vice Chairman, Union Carbide Corporation

WILLIAM S. OGDEN
Executive Vice President, The Chase Manhattan Bank, N.A.

WILLIAM R. PEARCE
Corporate Vice President, Cargill Incorporated

THOMAS A. REED
Group Vice President, International Control Systems, Honeywell Incorporated

NATHANIEL SAMUELS
Chairman, Louis Dreyfus Corporation; Limited Partner, Kuhn, Loeb & Company

DANIEL I. SARGENT
General Partner, Salomon Brothers

CHARLES R. SAYRE
President & General Manager, Staple Cotton Cooperative Association

MARK SHEPHERD, JR.
President, Texas Instruments, Incorporated

*LAUREN SOTH
West Des Moines, Iowa

WILLIAM F. SPENGLER
President and Chief Operating Officer, International Operations, Owens-Illinois

HENRY KING STANFORD
President, University of Miami

WALTER STERLING SURREY
Senior Partner, Surrey, Karasik & Morse

THOMAS N. URBAN
Vice President, Pioneer Hi-Bred International

CONSTANT M. van VLIERDEN
Executive Vice President, Bank of America N.T. & S.A.

OMER G. VOSS
Executive Vice President, International Harvester Company

GLENN E. WATTS
President, Communications Workers of America

*MARINA v. N. WHITMAN
Department of Economics, University of Pittsburgh

KEMMONS WILSON
Chairman of the Board, Holiday Inns, Incorporated

WILLIAM S. WOODSIDE
President, American Can Company

*See footnotes to the Statement.

# Acknowledgments

The authors acknowledge with gratitude the able assistance of their colleagues in the Citibank Economics Department; in particular, Margaret Beach, Ramachandra Bhagavatula, Thomas F. Huertas, K.S. Sri Kumar, James R. Lothian, Elizabeth Selvaggio, and Takuzo Yamada. The authors express their thanks to Marina v. N. Whitman of the University of Pittsburgh; to Donald J. Kahn and Ron Gold of the Exxon Corporation; to Neil McMullen of the National Planning Association; and to participants in the Lehrman Institute's Economic Policy Round Table, where an early version of part of this paper was presented. Other members of the Committee on Changing International Realities and its International Monetary Subcommittee also contributed many helpful criticisms and suggestions for improvement.

Harold van B. Cleveland
Vice President, Citibank
and W.H. Bruce Brittain
Assistant Vice President, Citibank

# Introduction 1

This report is about the Great Inflation of the early 1970s—how it happened, why it arose simultaneously in all parts of the industrial world and why inflation rates differed among countries to the extent they did. The subject is both vast and complex, but contemporary monetary theory, developed in part under the influence of this traumatic experience, helps to identify and resolve the major questions of causation and historical responsibility. The purpose of this report is to make certain insights and conclusions about the world inflation, derived from this body of theory, available to a public wider than the readers of professional economic journals.

The Great Inflation is not yet history. We are still too close to it—and the analytical tools and empirical studies are not yet available—to make a fully persuasive account of its causes possible. Nevertheless, we have attempted a preliminary explanation, knowing that our analysis and conclusions will be controversial and will doubtless require modification at some future time. It is in this tentative, undogmatic spirit that this essay is offered. The main arguments and conclusions of the report may be found in summary form in this chapter and in the Conclusion, which begins on page 49.

## WORLD INFLATION REACHES HIGH LEVELS

By comparison with the late 1960s and early 1970s, the early 1960s was a period of price stability. Between 1960 and 1965, consumer prices in the 10 leading industrial countries rose less than 2½ percent per annum and less than 1½ percent per annum in the United States. To contemporary observers, it appeared that the industrial countries were close to solving the problem of combining high levels of employment with reasonable stability of prices. Beginning in 1965, however, inflation began to accelerate, and from 1967 on it really took off, rising to a crescendo in 1974 when consumer prices in the 10 countries together increased no less than 13 percent.[1] Between the first quarter of 1968 and the fourth quarter of 1975, consumer prices rose 62 percent in the United States, 62 percent in Canada, 127 percent in Britain, 85 percent in France, 92 percent in Italy, and 106 percent in Japan, while at 47 percent, Germany's inflation was moderate only in a comparative sense.[2]

This was not, to be sure, the first time in this troubled century that world inflation had reached high levels. It did so immediately after the two world wars

1 The 10 countries are Belgium, Canada, France, Germany, Italy, Japan, the Netherlands, Switzerland, the United Kingdom, and the United States.

2 See Table 5-1 p. 26.

and briefly again in 1950–51 at the start of the Korean War. As in these earlier episodes, the world inflation of the early 1970s grew out of the exigencies of war finance—in this case, the inflationary financing by the United States of the war in Vietnam. Yet, the chain of economic events that led from the Johnson Administration's decision in 1965–67 to resort to the printing press for financing the war to the explosion of the world's money supply in 1971 and 1972 and the resulting inflationary crest in 1973–74 was largely unforeseen.

Indeed, the world inflation of the early 1970s was probably unforeseeable, given the then dominant economic theories which attributed inflation to local wage pressures or to other cost-push elements operating within separate national economies. As Harry Johnson put it in 1971, "[T]he problem of inflation has tended to appear in the literature as a series or collection of individual national problems, essentially sociological in origin, rather than as an international monetary problem."[3] Like the other great world monetary and economic trauma of modern times—the Great Depression—this disaster was the outcome of economic mechanisms operating on an international scale that might never have been allowed to work themselves out if they had been better understood at the time.

Like the Great Depression, too, the Great Inflation is likely to have lingering economic, political and social consequences. High and unsteady inflation has exacerbated social tensions within the industrial countries and sharpened conflict over income shares. Internationally, it has helped to raise tensions between poor nations and rich. Although the pace of price advances has come down from its 1974 peak, the leading industrial countries are now in a new period of monetary expansion and economic recovery that began with inflation several times greater than the 1-3 percent rate of the early 1960s. Demand management in the industrial countries may therefore continue to have a halting, stop-go character inimical to economic growth, as the struggle with rising prices is periodically renewed. Efforts to cope with inflation and its consequences by direct controls on prices, incomes and foreign exchange—efforts that seem to be continually renewed despite their repeated failure—may also affect growth adversely. Thus, conflicts over the distribution of income and wealth have been worsened by high and unstable inflation at a moment in history when the capacity of the economic machine to resolve them through rapid growth is threatened.

Another cost to the world community has been to impede effective international monetary cooperation. The inflationary experience of the late 1960s and early 1970s has eroded confidence in the feasibility of rules of international monetary behavior and in the key currency of the international monetary system, the U.S. dollar. It has heightened conflict among the industrial nations over exchange rates and commercial policy.

## MONETARY VS. NONMONETARY INFLATION THEORIES

This report, however, is not about the consequences of the Great Inflation but about its causes. We should make clear at the outset that we approach the subject from a particular theoretical standpoint—that of monetarism. "Inflation," as Mil-

3 Harry Johnson, *Inflation and the Monetarist Controversy* (Amsterdam-London, 1972), p. 9.

ton Friedman once put it, "is everywhere and at all times a monetary phenomenon," and doubtless few would disagree with the statement in this very general form.[4] For a sustained rise in the general level of prices must evidently be financed or validated by a sustained rise in the quantity of money in circulation relative to the need or demand for money. The general price level is, by definition, the total output of the economy, divided into its stock of money, multiplied by the velocity of circulation of money. Beyond this largely definitional agreement, however, contemporary theories of inflation divide sharply into two broad groups: monetary or monetarist theories and nonmonetary theories.

Monetary theories hold that high rates of money growth cause inflation. What connects high money supply growth rates to high inflation rates is the public's reaction to a change in the availability of money. When the quantity of money increases, the public reacts by spending more. This is because they have in mind a desired quantity of money which is, in part, determined by the volume of transactions they anticipate conducting. When the quantity of money supplied to the public by the central bank as currency and by the banking system as bank deposits (bank deposits are "money" because they can be readily used in exchange for goods) grows more quickly than the public's demand for money, the public treats the excess as a windfall and tries to spend more than their current receipts from production justify. Since people are trying to purchase more goods than are, in fact, being produced, goods are generally in short supply and their prices must rise. This is inflation.

The amount of inflation that results from an excess supply of money depends on how much faster the quantity of money supplied is growing than is the demand for money. If money demand grows by 4 percent a year while money supply grows at 10 percent a year, then prices ultimately rise at 6 percent a year. This growth of prices represents just enough inflation to reduce the growth of money supply, measured in real terms, to equal the growth of money demand.

An excess supply of money thus eventually leads to higher prices, but the process involves a long and somewhat variable time lag. In the case of the United States and the large industrial countries of Western Europe, the lag appears to be about two years. This lag is due mainly to the momentum of inflationary expectations. When a certain rate of inflation has persisted for some time, people expect it to continue, and they behave accordingly in setting prices and making wage bargains. As a result, when the public steps up its spending in response to an excess supply of money, the initial impact is not on prices and wages—which continue to advance at about the old rate—but on real economic activity and employment, which accordingly rise. In time, however, the additional demand in markets for goods, services and labor pushes prices and wages up. Expectations of future price rises will eventually also adjust upward, and equilibrium will be restored in markets for goods, services and labor at the new, higher rate of inflation.[5]

4 Milton Friedman, *The Counter-Revolution in Monetary Theory,* IEA Occasional Paper No. 33 (London, 1970).

5 Although changes in the supply of and the demand for money affect real economic activity in the short run, monetary theories hold that monetary factors have no substantial effect on the real growth rate in the longer run. Growth in the longer run is held to be determined by the growth of the capital stock and the labor force and by technological progress, which are, by and large, independent of monetary conditions.

The same process works in reverse when the supply of money falls relative to the demand for money. Since the public expects the going rate of inflation to continue, the first impact of the shortfall of money relative to demand is not on prices and costs but on business activity and employment, which accordingly fall. After a lag, prices and wages will respond to the weakness of demand in markets for goods, services and labor, and inflationary expectations will be adjusted downward. As this occurs, business activity rises and unemployment falls. It is important for some of the subsequent discussion to note that this recovery can take place naturally, without any new monetary or fiscal stimulus to the economy, simply as a consequence of the decline in the pace of inflation and the downward adjustment of price expectations.

Monetarist theories further hold that the supply of money is controlled by central banks, at least insofar as they are not fettered by such political considerations as fear of creating unemployment or pressure to help finance government deficits. Such theories also recognize that a country which fixes or stabilizes its exchange rate loses control of the domestic money supply to the balance of payments. The quantity of reserves its central bank can supply to the banking system (by intervening in the domestic money market or in the foreign exchange market) is largely governed by its commitment to defend a particular rate of exchange.

Nonmonetary theories of inflation agree that monetary expansion usually accompanies rising prices and is a necessary factor in inflation. But, they consider the role of the creators of money—the monetary authorities and the banking system—to be passive or merely responsive rather than active and potentially independent. The source of inflation, according to this view, is an exogenous upward movement of prices or wages, which the authorities and the banking system passively validate by monetary expansion. The upward movement of prices or wages is not simply a consequence of excess demand for goods and labor, and of inflationary expectations, as monetary theories hold. It is more fundamentally a result of social or political causes such as dissatisfaction with existing income distribution, or the exercise of monopoly power by firms or trade unions. The monetary authority is assumed to respond passively to the increased demand for credit caused by the exogenous rise in prices and costs.

Those economists who hold this view "agree with [J.R.] Hicks that our present troubles are not of a monetary character and are not to be cured by monetary means, and that whilst 'it was true in the old days that inflation was a monetary matter, prices rose because the supply of money was greater than the demand for it . . . money is now a mere counter, which is supplied by the banking system (or by the government through the banking system) just as it is required.' Some would go even further and agree with [R.F.] Harrod that the 'new wage-price explosion is altogether unprecedented. . . . The causes are sociological [and] first cousins to the causes of such things as student unrest.'"[6] Such views are widely held in Britain, France and Italy—countries where the central bank has been subject to serious political constraints in holding down money growth and has more often than not followed an accommodating monetary policy of the kind these theories presuppose.

6 D. Laidler and M. Parkin, "Inflation: A Survey," *The Economic Journal* (December 1975), p. 741.

Monetary and nonmonetary approaches are in agreement that, in the inflationary process, the rise of prices and costs takes on a life of its own, independent of the initial cause. The monetarist theories attribute it to inflationary expectations, while the nonmonetary theories see it as a self-contained upward spiral, in which prices respond to wages and wages to prices and so on, indefinitely. The two approaches also agree that monetary policy plays a part—active in one case, passive in the other—in maintaining inflation. But, despite such areas of partial agreement, the two approaches yield policy conclusions that are diametrically opposed. Nonmonetary theories point to the need for price and wage controls. But, as such controls have not worked well in a democratic context, these theories lead to the conclusion that the root causes of inflation are probably beyond the reach of policy. Monetary theories are more sanguine. They imply that inflation can be reduced to tolerable proportions by slowing the rate of money growth to a pace consistent with the desired rate of inflation. If this were done gradually enough—perhaps in several discrete steps over a period of years—the cost in lost output and unemployment could be small enough to remain within politically tolerable bounds.

Inflation normally involves a vicious circle in which excessive monetary expansion leads to higher prices, and higher prices to higher claims for wages, which lead in turn to more monetary expansion. For the monetarist, the problem can in principle be solved if the circle can be broken at the monetary link. Then, in an economic environment of diminishing inflation, wage demands will also acquire their own downward momentum, reducing the political pressure on the authorities to continue excessive money growth.

## PUBLIC SPENDING, BUDGET DEFICITS AND INFLATION

In the last decade, some of the European countries have exhibited a tendency to inflation that cannot be explained without recourse to an analysis which is as much sociological and political as monetary. The pressure of powerful social groups demanding more real income, improved social benefits and greater security of employment has led to a growth of public spending more rapid than the growth of the national income. Moreover, in a number of countries—Italy is the outstanding example—real wages have risen more rapidly than the real national income during the past decade. This has squeezed the financial resources of companies in the private sector as well as in nationalized industries, particularly where price controls or rate regulation have kept prices from rising as rapidly as costs. The resulting need to subsidize companies in financial trouble has been a further important drain on the public purse. In these circumstances, budgets both national and municipal have tended to fall into chronic deficit, which has made heavy public borrowing necessary. Such large borrowing requirements have become an endemic source of inflation. For noninflationary public borrowing on the scale required would raise real interest rates and crowd out some of the private borrowing on which economic growth depends. Governments and their central banks have therefore been prone to follow expansive monetary policies in an effort to accommodate heavy public and private demands for credit that would otherwise exceed the supply.

A structural and political analysis of this kind helps explain a tendency to excessive monetary expansion and inflation in some of the European countries. Yet, it sheds little light on the two outstanding facts about the Great Inflation: namely, the rapidity of its onslaught and its simultaneous appearance worldwide. Nor can the theories that attribute inflation to an exogenous wage-price spiral explain the sudden intensification of inflation that occurred in all countries simultaneously in the mid-1960s. For the social forces and institutional structures that are supposed to cause the spiral change slowly and in different societies at different times.

The focus of this report is on inflation as an international process. It leans heavily on the body of theory known as the monetary theory of the balance of payments.[7] This theory seeks to explain the interconnections between national money supplies and price levels in an open international system such as that linking the Western industrial countries. The theory is explained in the next chapter, with particular emphasis on the central role of the U.S. Federal Reserve System in influencing the world's money supply and the world's price level. Propositions derived from this theory are compared with the facts—the experience of the main industrial countries in the period 1967–75. An explanation of world inflation that deals with inflation's monetary causes is incomplete without an explanation of *why* national authorities made the decisions that caused or allowed money and prices to get out of hand. In the penultimate section of the report, we look more directly at these decisions, the political constraints and pressures involved and the economic arguments used to justify, or rationalize, them. The final chapter brings together the report's main conclusions.

---

7 Major contemporary proponents of this approach are Robert A. Mundell (see his *Monetary Theory: Inflation, Interest and Growth in the World Economy,* Pacific Palisades, 1971) and Harry Johnson (see his "The Monetary Approach to Balance of Payments Theory," *Journal of Financial and Quantitative Analysis,* March 1972; and *Inflation and the Monetarist Controversy,* Amsterdam-London, 1972.) See also Rudiger Dornbusch, "Devaluation, Money and Non-Traded Goods," *American Economic Review* (December 1973), and Jacob A. Frenkel, "Adjustment Mechanisms and the Monetary Approach to the Balance of Payments," E. Classen and P. Salin, eds., *Recent Issues in International Monetary Economics* (Amsterdam, 1976).

For an excellent, comprehensive overview of this theory and its relationship to earlier views of the balance of payments, see Marina v. N. Whitman, "Global Monetarism and the Monetary Approach to the Balance of Payments," *Papers on Economic Activity* (Washington, D.C.: Brookings Institution, 1976), p. 491. "Global monetarism," as Professor Whitman has dubbed it, has long historical roots. It derives in part from the price-specie flow mechanism, conventionally attributed to the Scottish classical economist David Hume, and from the purchasing-power parity theorem, generally attributed to Gustav Cassel, who wrote in the early 1900s. Another dimension of the theory, which describes the role of a reserve currency, seems to have been first described by the French economists Jacques Rueff and Albert Aftalion in the early 1930s. See, e.g., Aftalion, "The Causes and Effects of the Movements of Gold into France," *Selected Documents of the Gold Delegation* (Geneva: League of Nations, 1931), p. 8; Rueff, "The Case for the Gold Standard" (Lecture delivered in Paris in 1932), in *The Age of Inflation* (Chicago, 1964), pp. 51–52.

# World Money and World Inflation 2

A monetary account of the Great Inflation must be able to explain both the similarity and the diversity of inflationary experience. At first blush, it is diversity rather than the similarity that strikes the eye. In the period 1968–75, Britain's inflation was more than double U.S. inflation. In France, Italy and Japan, prices rose half again as much as did U.S. prices, while prices in Germany and the small industrial countries of continental Europe rose somewhat less than did prices in the United States. Among the leading industrial countries, rates of inflation in the 1968–75 period, measured by consumer prices, were approximately equal only in Canada and the United States.[1] Yet, what stands out in the Great Inflation is not that inflations differed among countries—that had also been true earlier—but rather that prices rose so much more swiftly everywhere after the mid-1960s than before. It is this common element in the experience of the industrial countries—suggesting as it does some common monetary factor simultaneously at work everywhere—that must first be explained, if we are to understand the Great Inflation.

## COMMON PRICE LEVEL AND COMMON MONEY STOCK

In an international monetary system of fixed exchange rates, individual countries' money supplies are linked via the balance of payments and their price levels are linked via competition and arbitrage in markets for goods and services. In such a system, there is for practical purposes a common "world" money supply and a common "world" price level. A simple, hypothetical example will serve to demonstrate how the common price level and the common money stock are determined in an integrated economic world.

Let us begin from a position of monetary equilibrium, in which all countries' money stocks are growing at the same rate as the demand for money and prices are stable. Suppose that in one of the larger countries, the authorities decide that the money supply should be increased, in order to lower interest rates and stimulate business activity. The central bank accordingly expands the monetary base by expanding domestic credit—i.e., by increasing its domestic assets by, for example, open market purchases of Treasury bills or by extending credit to commercial banks. The money supply expands in the same proportion as the monetary base (assuming no change in the money multiplier).[2] The result is a temporary excess

---

1 See Table 5-1, p. 26.

2 The monetary base is conventionally defined as the sum of currency in circulation and the reserve deposits of commercial banks with the central bank. The money supply, defined as the sum of currency in circulation and the public's deposits with commercial banks, normally has a fairly stable relationship—the money multiplier—with the monetary base. The central bank can increase or reduce the monetary base by adding to or reducing its portfolio of domestic assets or foreign assets (gold and financial assets denominated in foreign currencies).

supply of money relative to the demand for money in the country.

Part of the excess money is spent at home, putting downward pressure on interest rates, raising domestic incomes and ultimately raising domestic prices. A part of the excess is also spent abroad on goods, services and capital. This part causes the central bank's reserves of gold and foreign currencies to decline, thereby reducing *pro tanto* the country's monetary base and tending to reduce the excess supply of money as well.

Since exchange rates are fixed, second countries end up importing inflation from the first country as they simultaneously experience upward pressure on price levels and additional monetary expansion. One source of increased money growth is first-country residents' increased expenditures on second-country goods and capital. This puts excess money in the hands of residents of the second country, and this, in turn, increases spending on domestic goods, putting upward pressure on the second country's price level.

Furthermore, the rise in prices of internationally traded goods in the first country provides a direct, competitive reason for domestic producers in the second country to raise their own prices. If they do not, they will lose profits to international arbitragers who will buy traded goods at low prices in the second country and sell them at high prices in the first country. Domestic goods prices will rise sympathetically with traded goods prices in the second country, as producers there shift to producing more internationally traded goods and as consumers in the second country cut back purchases of internationally traded goods in favor of domestically produced goods. The final result is upward pressure on domestic goods prices in the second country from both sides of the market.

This upward pressure on all prices in the second (inflation-importing) country may lead to further money growth there. Higher prices in the second country lower the real value of cash balances below their desired level. A balance-of-payments surplus that draws more funds—and reserves—from the first country to the second is one way second-country residents can reconstitute their real cash balances. Thus, a complex mechanism operating via the balance of payments and through markets for goods and services restores monetary equilibrium in both countries.

When adjustment is complete, the general level of prices in all countries will be higher by an amount proportional to the initial increase in the first country's money supply divided by the initial money supply of all countries taken together. In other words, the initial excess supply of money will have been redistributed, via the balance of payments, among the whole group of countries in proportion to their respective money supplies. It will accordingly have raised prices in each country by the same proportion, which is the ratio of the initial excess supply of money in the first country to the initial "world" money supply.[3]

## WORLD MONEY AND WORLD PRICES, 1960-71

Between 1960 and 1971, before exchange-rate stability began to break down, the industrial countries as a group constituted a "world" of the kind just described

3 To simplify the exposition, we have assumed that the demand for money is constant. If the demand for money had risen in the interim, because of a rise in real income, for example, the final world price level would be lower.

**CHART 2-1**

**World Inflation Follows World Money Growth**

Note: World money and world inflation are three-quarter moving averages of the aggregated annualized money and price growth rates for Belgium, Canada, France, Germany, Italy, Japan, the Netherlands, Switzerland, the United Kingdom, and the United States. The world money supply (M1) is the sum of individual countries' narrowly defined money stocks (M1) converted at 1971 exchange rates. World inflation is the sum of individual countries' inflation rates weighted according to each countries' share of the world money supply.

Source: Appendix Tables.

in theoretical terms. Exchange rates were mostly fixed and relatively stable and trade and capital movements were relatively free. Controls on trade and capital movements were changing in this period, and there were several changes in exchange rates among leading currencies.[4] But, such changes were probably not large enough to make a broad comparison between this real world and the analytical model invalid.

---

4 The German mark and the Dutch guilder were revalued in 1961 and again in 1969, and the Canadian dollar was devalued in 1962, sterling was devalued in 1967 and the French franc in 1969.

Chart 2-1 makes such a comparison. It brings out the association between the general acceleration of prices from 1967 on and the acceleration of the money supply in the industrial countries as a group. The chart plots a three-quarter moving average of the aggregate money stock in the 10 largest countries and a three-quarter moving average of prices in these countries. The money stock was calculated as the sum of the 10 countries' narrowly defined money stocks, expressed in dollars at 1971 exchange rates. The consumer price index was calculated using the same countries' consumer price indices weighted by their shares in total world gross national product, also aggregated at 1971 exchange rates. Quite clearly, the marked accelerations in inflation in the period 1968–69 and again in 1973–75 are preceded by marked accelerations in money growth, approximately two years earlier. And, the general upward trend in the rate of inflation over the whole period shown is associated with a similar upward trend in the pace of monetary expansion. Since monetary theory suggests that a lagged relationship of the kind shown in the chart should hold between world money and world prices, it seems reasonable to believe that the relationship observed is, in fact, one of cause and effect.

While the acceleration of world money and the resulting strong pressure of demand on supply played a big part in the Great Inflation, it is widely thought that monetary expansion was only one of several major causes.[5] In particular, exogenous changes in supply conditions—including the decision of the Organization of Petroleum Exporting Countries (OPEC) to raise oil prices, and poor harvests in the Soviet Union and the United States—are thought to have raised world prices much higher than can be accounted for by monetary causes. Properly understood, this is probably true. The major changes in supply conditions affecting food and energy prices probably affected the timing of the rise in the world price level, helping to account for the steep run up of the price level in 1973 and 1974. But, it is a different question whether exogenous changes in supply conditions affected the final level of world prices—i.e., total inflation over the period 1968–75.

Theory suggests that changes in supply conditions, such as the actions of OPEC, can raise the general level of prices in the short run but cannot raise the price level permanently. Suppose, for instance, that in a country where the price level has been stable, the price of energy is raised by the OPEC cartel. In the short run, the general level of prices will rise. This rise will tend to create a shortage of real cash balances, assuming no intervening change in the nominal money stock. This shortage will exert downward pressure on the general price level, and this pressure will continue until the general price level is back to its initial level. In other words, in the longer run, the general or aggregate level of prices is determined by the supply of and the demand for money, not by the supply of and the demand for particular goods or services. When the adjustment is complete, the price of energy and energy-intensive products will be higher in terms of other products, but the absolute level of prices generally will be the same as it would have been—with monetary conditions given—if the change of the OPEC oil price had never occurred.

---

5 Extensive theoretical and empirical work on world inflation and its transmission among the developed countries is reported in M. Parkin and G. Zis, eds., *Inflation in the World Economy* (Manchester, 1976).

To test this theoretical point, we did a simple statistical analysis of money-stock levels and prices in the industrial countries. The analysis showed that in 1975, the price level in the 10 countries was lower—not higher—than the price level that would have been predicted with the existing money supply and the estimated demand for money in real terms in those countries.[6] This probably means that by 1975, the world price level had not yet fully adjusted to the increase in money that had occurred up to that time. It also suggests that exogenous supply factors probably did not have a major independent influence on the total rise in the world price level over the period 1968–75, although as noted, supply factors probably contributed to the acceleration of inflation in 1973–74. However, as noted, the rise in oil prices and other supply-induced price increases probably contributed to the acceleration of inflation in 1973–74. They may also have continued to influence the world price level beyond the period covered by our analysis.

6 We calculated the trend of velocity of the narrowly defined money supply, M1, in 10 industrial countries by regressing the log of velocity on time for several different subperiods (all ending in 1967). We then projected these trends through 1975, multiplied the trend value by the quantity of money (M1) then in circulation and divided by the level of real income to obtain estimates of the price level implied by underlying monetary conditions. Regardless of the period chosen for the trend calculation, implied prices were consistently above actual prices. The data were taken from Appendix Tables A-1, A-2 and A-3.

# Where Did the Money Come From? 3

In the model of world inflation and fixed exchange rates outlined in Chapter 2, we suggested that the increase in world money supply was the combined result of an increase in central bank credit in one or more countries and its transmission to other countries via the balance of payments. If the monetary system is one in which central banks hold their reserves primarily in gold, and hold reserve assets denominated in foreign currencies only as working balances that are convertible on demand into gold, the increase in the world money supply resulting from an expansion of domestic credit in one country is unlikely to be large. For the initial excess supply of money in the system, although perhaps large relative to the money supply of the country responsible for it, is apt to be small relative to the total world money supply. This is because in a system in which the rule of gold convertibility prevails, no country is likely to have reserves of gold and foreign currencies large enough to raise the world money supply rapidly over an extended period of time. If it tried, its reserves would soon be depleted. In such a system, rapid, prolonged inflation is therefore unlikely, because domestic credit expansion and world money growth are limited by the world's supply of monetary gold and by the unwillingness of central banks to accumulate holdings of foreign currencies beyond their normal needs for working balances.

Until the Bretton Woods system reached its full development in the early 1960s, international monetary systems had normally been governed by the rule of gold convertibility, except in major wars. Under the gold-exchange standard in the 1920s and even to a smaller extent under the classical gold standard, some central banks were accustomed to hold foreign currencies—mainly sterling—as international reserves. But, the reserve currencies were themselves freely convertible into gold at the demand of central banks or private parties. Thus, credit expansion and money growth were still ultimately tied to the aggregate supply of monetary gold in the system. This, of course, is why, until the Great Inflation, rapid, prolonged inflation on an international scale occurred only as a result of major wars, when convertibility was restricted or suspended.[1]

World inflation of the sort we have experienced in recent years presupposes an international monetary system in which the rule of convertibility has been suspended, and at least one large country is able consistently to expand domestic

---

1 In the 1930s, the gold convertibility of all major currencies was suspended at one time or another. But, as this occurred during a period when exchange rates of the leading currencies were floating, and when countries were not pursuing inflationary domestic credit policies, the experience is not directly relevant to the present discussion of inflation under a fixed-rate regime. For a recent review of monetary policies and the international monetary system in the 1920s and 1930s, see Harold van B. Cleveland, "The International Monetary System in the Interwar Period," in B. Rowland, ed., *Balance of Power or Hegemony: The Interwar Monetary System* (New York, 1976).

credit and create money in excess of the local demand for it, without losing international reserves. The system must be such that this country neither loses reserves nor tends to reduce its domestic monetary base when it incurs an overall payments deficit. Other countries will hold a large part of their reserves in financial assets denominated in the currency of the reserve center, rather than in gold, and they will peg their currencies to the reserve currency, maintaining the pegged rates by intervening in the exchange markets to buy or sell their currencies against the reserve currency. Other countries will generally refrain from converting holdings of the reserve currency into gold, even if formal convertibility exists, and the reserve center will accept no responsibility to maintain the exchange rates of its currency against other currencies.

The monetary system that evolved after World War II within the framework of the Articles of Agreement of the International Monetary Fund—known as the Bretton Woods system—had all these characteristics. Although the dollar remained formally convertible into gold for official international settlements until August 1971, convertibility became increasingly fictitious as U.S. dollar liabilities to foreigners and foreign central banks grew. From the early 1960s on, the legal possibility and occasional fact of official gold conversions were not a major limitation on U.S. domestic monetary policy. And, by the beginning of the period of the Great Inflation, convertibility had been virtually suspended *de facto* (in March 1968), as the system became a nearly pure dollar standard. Thereafter, the U.S. gold reserve and monetary base were almost completely insulated from the U.S. balance of payments.

## THE RESERVE-CURRENCY MECHANISM

To see the monetary consequences of these institutional arrangements, suppose that the United States experiences a balance-of-payments deficit that is financed by a check drawn on a New York bank. The check will be sold to a foreign central bank in return for that country's money. If the U.S. dollar were like any other currency, this transaction would reduce the reserves of the American banking system and force contraction of the U.S. money stock. But, since the dollar serves as international reserves, the foreign central bank would hold the increased dollars, probably in the form of an interest-bearing dollar asset such as a certificate of deposit, or a U.S. Treasury bill purchased in the U.S. money market. The sale by the central bank of the dollar check for a certificate of deposit or a Treasury bill would reconstitute the reserves of the U.S. banking system and cancel out the initial, contractionary effect of the payments outflow on the monetary base.

It might seem that any country could have asserted its monetary independence of the United States simply by expanding or contracting domestic credit to offset ("sterilize") the effect of reserve changes on its money supply. Indeed, U.S. officials frequently advanced this argument during the period under review in reply to European accusations that the United States was exporting inflation via its balance-of-payments deficit. But, a sterilization policy could not have been ultimately effective, for it would have perpetuated the disequilibrium in the country's balance of payments. Since the flow of funds from dollars to the other currency had no tendency to reduce the U.S. money supply, the flow could continue indefinitely as long as monetary conditions in the country differed from those in the United States. Sterilization of inflows would simply have maintained the difference in monetary conditions that caused the flow. The result would have been to undermine confidence in the stability of the exchange rate and to force the country, if it desired to maintain the parity of its currency, to bring its monetary policy back into line with that of the United States. In sum, under the Bretton Woods system the Federal Reserve functioned (albeit unwittingly) as a world central bank.

## MONETARY LEADERSHIP

We have described the operation of the Bretton Woods system as though the increase in other countries' money supplies was brought about primarily by increases in their dollar reserves, arising out of a U.S. balance-of-payments deficit. This was in fact a principal way in which other countries' money supplies were increased during the period of the Great Inflation. But, the United States also influenced monetary conditions in other countries under the Bretton Woods system through another mechanism, which may be called monetary leadership.[2] This mechanism played an important part in the earlier stages of the world inflation in the period up to 1969, when the U.S. payments deficit was still relatively small.

Suppose that a central bank follows a consistent policy of keeping local short-term interest rates aligned on interest rates in the United States or in the Eurodollar market, in order to help stabilize its exchange rate with the dollar, as many countries customarily did in the 1960s. The central bank accomplishes this result by expanding domestic credit when local interest rates tend to rise relative to U.S. or Eurodollar interest rates, and by contracting domestic credit when local interest rates tend to fall relative to dollar interest rates. The consequence of this policy will be that domestic monetary conditions in the country will tend to remain in line with those in the United States. This will be accomplished not by virtue of changes in the local central bank's international reserves, but rather via changes in its domestic assets.

To see how this works, assume that short-term interest rates in the United States fall because the Federal Reserve has embarked on a more expansive monetary policy. In order to stabilize interest rates in the United Kingdom at the level of interest rates in the United States and keep the pound from rising against the dollar, the Bank of England pursues expansive open market operations, expanding Britain's monetary base. As a result, Britain's money supply also begins to grow more rapidly, and the exchange rate is stabilized. Or, suppose that business activity accelerates in the United Kingdom. This brings about an increase in the demand for credit and a rise in British interest rates relative to U.S. rates. In order to keep the pound from rising, the Bank of England buys Treasury bills, to bring British rates back down to the U.S. level. This increases the British money supply, satisfying the increased demand for credit, and bringing British interest rates back down. Again, the result is to stabilize the exchange rate between the pound and the

2 For a discussion of "shared" leadership in the international monetary system, see R. McKinnon, "A New Tripartite Monetary Agreement or a Limping Dollar Standard," Essays in International Finance, No. 106 (Princeton University, International Finance Section, October 1964).

dollar. In both examples, stabilization comes from intervention in the domestic money market rather than intervention in the exchange market.

In sum, if the Bank of England wants to stabilize the pound-dollar exchange rate, it can do so by intervening in the domestic money market or in the exchange market. But, in the longer run, it cannot choose how fast its monetary base and money supply will grow. This will depend not on what the Bank of England does but rather on the demand for money in Britain and the pace of monetary expansion in the United States. Any divergence between monetary conditions in Britain and the United States that the Bank of England allows to arise will be corrected, sooner or later, by an inflow or outflow of funds via the balance of payments. The flows will alter Britain's monetary base through their effect on the Bank of England's reserves.

The United States, in our example, is under no such compulsion to intervene in the exchange market, or to align U.S. interest rates on foreign rates, in order to stabilize the exchange rate of the dollar. The Federal Reserve can set U.S. interest rates at any level it chooses (in the short run), regardless of interest rates abroad, by expanding or contracting domestic credit. If as a result U.S. interest rates rise or fall relative to foreign interest rates, the United States will have a balance-of-payments surplus or deficit. But, as already explained, this will have no tendency to discipline U.S. monetary policy or to alter the U.S. monetary base. Rather, it will force other central banks either to intervene in the exchange markets, or to conform their interest rates to U.S. rates if they wish to keep their currencies stable against the dollar. In either case, the Federal Reserve leads and other central banks follow.

It should be noted that the ability of the Federal Reserve to influence world monetary conditions does not depend on exchange rates being formally pegged to the dollar. It is sufficient if other central banks customarily stabilize their currencies against the dollar, whether they do so by intervening in the exchange markets or by aligning domestic interest rates on dollar rates.

For this reason, the foregoing model of the dollar standard applies both to the Bretton Woods system and to the system of managed floating that followed the abandonment of fixed exchange rates. In the managed float, some countries continued to stabilize their currencies against the dollar by some combination of domestic monetary policy and intervention in the exchange markets. For example, the Canadian dollar has not been pegged to the U.S. dollar since June 1970, but the Bank of Canada has followed a monetary policy aimed at keeping the Canadian dollar close to par with the U.S. dollar over the longer run, occasionally intervening in the exchange market for the same purpose. Over time, the result is about the same as if the Bank of Canada pegged the Canadian dollar to the U.S. dollar.

# U.S. Money and World Money 4

The preceding discussion of the reserve-currency mechanism showed how U.S. monetary policy may have influenced monetary conditions in other countries under the Bretton Woods system. Our argument is that the strong acceleration of U.S. money growth and inflation in the late 1960s and early 1970s was probably the principal cause of the industrial world's Great Inflation. Chart 4-1 summarizes statistical evidence tending to support the view that, under the Bretton Woods system, monetary expansion and price inflation in the other industrial countries was causally connected with monetary expansion and inflation in the United States.

The analysis that underlies the chart implies that there is a consistent pattern of time lags between changes in U.S. monetary conditions and changes in monetary conditions in the other nine leading industrial countries in the period 1954–71. A country's "monetary conditions" were defined as the rate of growth of the country's narrowly defined money supply (M1), minus the trend growth rate of its real gross national product. The latter variable serves as a proxy for the growth of the demand for money. According to this analysis, changes in U.S. monetary conditions precede changes in monetary conditions in the other nine countries. In a statistical sense, most of the influence of U.S. monetary conditions on conditions in the other countries occurs with a lag of four to eight quarters. This pattern is consistent with the view that U.S. monetary policy tends to shape world monetary conditions in the longer run, when exchange rates are fixed.

Moreover, the observed lag is consistent with the transmission mechanism previously described. The mechanism includes the direct effects of U.S. balance-of-payments deficits and U.S. monetary policy on foreign money supplies, and the effects of U.S. prices on foreign prices. When the U.S. money supply begins to grow more rapidly, the effect on spending in the United States is felt mostly within a period of zero to four quarters. The direct effect on the U.S. balance of payments—tending to cause an overall deficit—would accordingly be felt in about the same period. Likewise, the effect of more rapid U.S. money growth on the U.S. price level is mostly complete in a period of eight calendar quarters.[1] Accordingly, the sympathetic rise in foreign prices, induced by the rise in U.S. prices, should occur with a similar lag. The observed zero to eight quarter lag between changes in U.S. and foreign monetary conditions therefore seems consistent with the inflation-transmission mechanism sketched above.

U.S. inflation in the period from first quarter 1968 to fourth quarter 1975 was 62 percent. In the same period, inflation in the nine other leading industrial countries

1 See, e.g., Milton Friedman, "The Lag in the Effect of Monetary Policy," in *The Optimum Quantity of Money and other Essays*" (Chicago, 1969), pp. 237–260.

## CHART 4-1

### Time Lags Between Money Growth Rates of the United States and a Group of Nine Other Countries, 1954–71

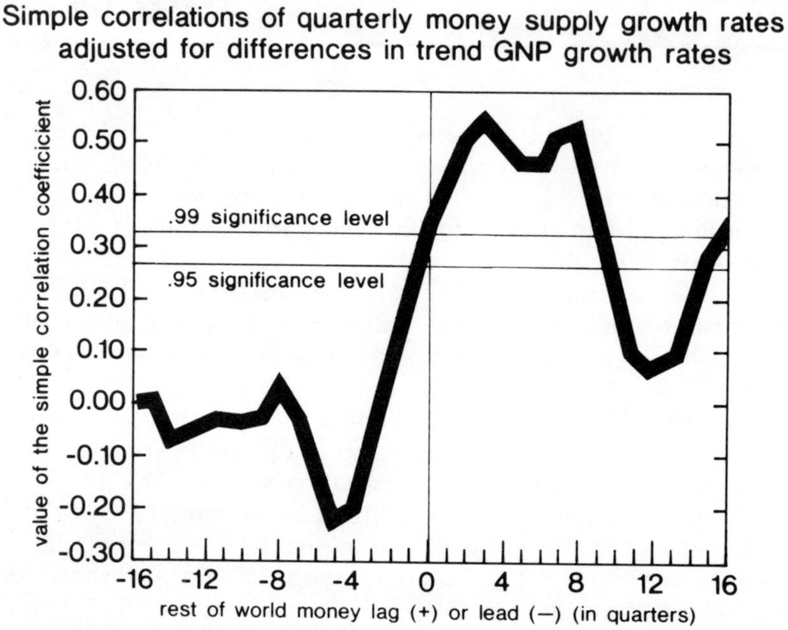


Note: The correlation coefficient measures how closely matched are changes in U.S. adjusted money growth rates and adjusted money growth of the nine. If the correlation coefficient is positive, the nine's money growth rate has tended to rise with the U.S. growth rate. If the correlation coefficient is negative, increases in the adjusted U.S. money growth rate have been associated with decreases in the nine's adjusted money growth rates. The figure shows that the association between current U.S. adjusted money growth rates and the nine's adjusted growth rates from four to eight quarters later are positively correlated or that increases in U.S. adjusted money growth rates are associated with increases in the nine's adjusted money growth rates from 4 to 8 quarters later. However, correlations of U.S. adjusted money growth with past rates of growth of the nine's adjusted money stock and with the nine's growth rate from 0-3 quarters later and more than 8 quarters later are indistinguishable from 0. This is shown by the lines designated ".95 and .99 significance level." When a positive correlation coefficient is less than the value indicated by these lines, it cannot be distinguished from 0. The correlation coefficients are less than one, which means that growth of the adjusted U.S. money stock is less than a full explanation of adjusted rest-of-world money growth. Factors other than U.S. money must therefore have influenced the quarterly rest-of-world money growth rates. But, the positive correlation coefficients are evidence that changes in U.S. money growth preceded changes in money growth in the rest of the world.

Source: Appendix Tables.

was 86 percent.[2] Our analysis implies that U.S. money growth was responsible for the major part of the Great Inflation. Gottfried Haberler was close to the mark when he wrote recently that "[u]nder the dollar standard . . . the world price level (more precisely the price level of the many countries that pegged their currencies to the dollar) was virtually determined by the U.S. price level. That is to say, world inflation was made in the United States."[3]

## OTHER VIEWS

The major role U.S. monetary policy played in world money growth and world inflation is not yet widely accepted, so the reader may wish to consider alternative explanations of the world money explosion of the late 1960s and early 1970s.

One view is that the real culprit was the massive increase that occurred in the dollar reserves of other countries, particularly in 1971, 1972 and early 1973, as money managers fled from the dollar in anticipation of an upward movement of European currencies and the yen against the dollar. In these terms, the loss of confidence in the dollar appears to be the proximate cause of world inflation. As the point is sometimes put, speculation or hedging against a devaluation of the dollar converted low-powered money (privately held dollar balances) into high-powered base money, as the European and Japanese central banks bought dollars on the exchange markets to hold their currencies down against the dollar. The resulting rapid expansion of money in Europe and Japan was, according to this view, responsible for inflation there.[4] The Eurodollar market is singled out for particular opprobrium in this explanation because it was an important means of financing short-term positions against the dollar and in favor of other currencies. This explanation of inflation has been current in European financial circles.[5] For example, in its report for the year 1971, the Bundesbank complained of an "influx that increasingly swamped the German monetary system with steadily growing inflationary effects."[6]

---

2 Inflation in the nine countries was aggregated for the purpose of this comparison by weighting the percentage increase in national consumer price indices over the 1968–75 period by the dollar values of their respective gross national products, computed at average 1971 rates of exchange. The price data are from Appendix Table A-1.

3 Gottfried Haberler, "Inflation as a World-wide Phenomenon," in D. Meiselman and A. Laffer, eds., *The Phenomenon of Worldwide Inflation* (Washington, D.C., 1975), p. 15.

4 For example, "[I]t has been argued that an excessive monetary expansion in the United States was the main cause of the increase in world liquidity and the ensuing worldwide inflation. However, there is not much convincing evidence to support this notion. In fact, during 1970–72, the increase in the money supply in the United States was more moderate than in any other industrial country. Instead, a shift by U.S. and foreign private entities out of dollars and into other currencies led to an excessive expansion of global liquidity in the early 1970s." H. Heller, "International Reserves, Money and Global Inflation," *Finance and Development* (Washington, D.C.: World Bank, March 1976), p. 28.

5 See, e.g., O. Emminger, *Inflation and the International Monetary System* (Washington, D.C.: The Per Jacobson Foundation, 1973), *passim*.

6 Deutsche Bundesbank, Annual Report for the Year 1971, p. 30.

There is a measure of truth in singling out hedging or speculation against the dollar as a source of world inflation. Such speculative flows did enlarge the monetary base and the money supply in European countries, as well as in Japan. In fact, inflows of dollars, partly speculative in character, were responsible for much of the increase in other industrial countries' monetary bases in the years 1970–73 (see Chart 4-2). But, it is a different question whether the inflows caused the money supply and price inflation in these countries to be greater than they otherwise would have been. Monetary theory suggests that this was probably not the case. Inflation occurs when there is an excess of money supply over the demand for money. The inflows of funds occurred in response to a new, speculative demand for marks. Thus, it was the increase in demand for marks that gave rise to the increase in the supply of marks; therefore, the inflows could not have created or

**CHART 4-2**

**Sources of the Aggregate Monetary Base for Nine Industrialized Countries**

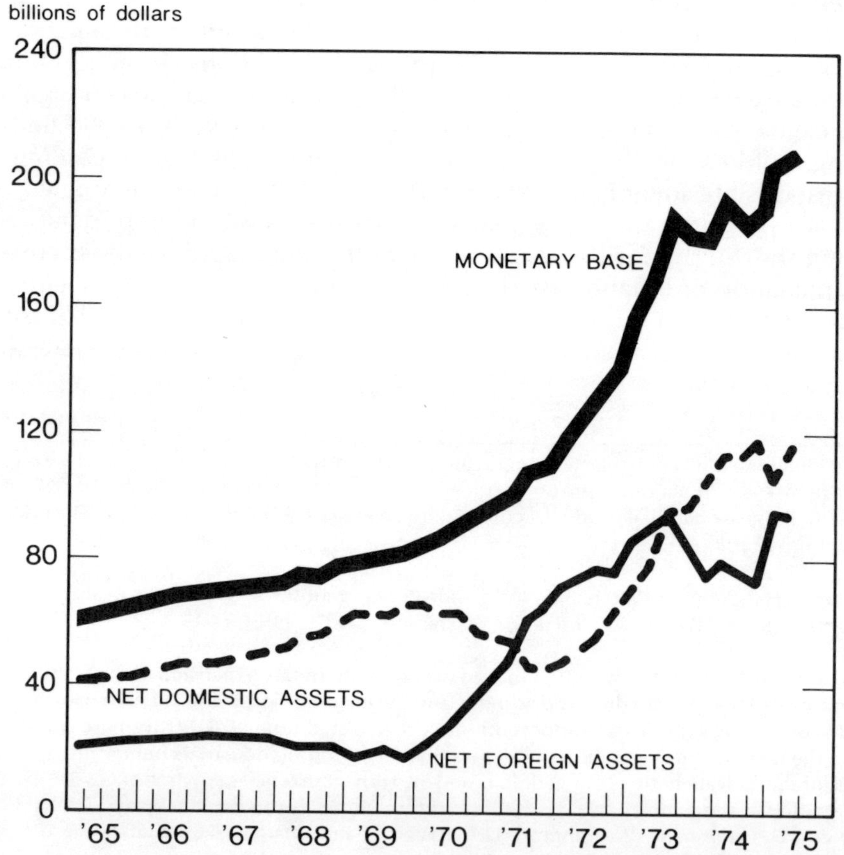


Note: The nine countries included are Belgium, Canada, France, Germany, Italy, Japan, the Netherlands, Switzerland, and the United Kingdom. The components were aggregated using current exchange rates.

Source: IMF International Financial Statistics and the Federal Reserve Bulletin.

contributed to creating an excess of mark money supply over demand. How, then, could they have raised German prices above the level they otherwise would have reached?

More precisely, the model of world inflation under fixed exchange rates outlined above suggests that speculative inflows would not have altered the German price level. According to the model, under fixed exchange rates, the price level in countries other than the United States is determined in the longer run by U.S. monetary conditions. With the exchange rate fixed, the German money supply would therefore be determined by the demand for money in Germany, including the additional money needed to validate inflation imported from the United States. If this money demand had not been satisfied by inflows that occurred as a consequence of currency hedging or speculation, it would have been satisfied by a normal surplus in the German balance of payments, or by more domestic credit expansion in Germany.

It is significant that the countries whose currencies were the prime speculative targets in the early 1970s—Germany and Switzerland—also had the least inflation. The connection between the two facts is clear. The German and Swiss authorities' greater concern about inflation caused them to follow more restrictive domestic monetary policies than other countries, and made them likely, in the view of the markets, to upvalue their currencies. Accordingly, these currencies became attractive to money managers. If currency speculation was a main cause of inflation, Germany and Switzerland should have had more inflation than other European countries, not less as they did.

In theory, the only way currency speculation against the dollar could have affected world prices in the longer run is by reducing the demand for dollars. To see this, suppose that with the exchange rate fixed, a private holder of dollars decides to buy marks because he anticipates a rise in the mark against the dollar. This would cause the Bundesbank to acquire dollars in exchange for marks, thereby increasing the German monetary base and the German money supply. As suggested above, this would have no direct effect on the German price level, at least in the longer run. But, there would be a possible indirect effect on German prices because there is a possible effect on the U.S. price level.

The speculative shift from dollars to marks reflects an increase in the demand for marks and a decrease in the demand for dollars. Decreased dollar demand, given a constant quantity of dollars in circulation, means that dollar prices must rise. But, because the U.S. money supply is much larger than the German money supply, the proportionate impact on U.S. prices—and therefore indirectly on German prices—is much smaller than is suggested by comparing the size of the speculative inflow with the German monetary base. The effect on U.S. prices—and German prices—would be even smaller if the shift was mainly or entirely out of U.S. securities or other financial instruments of a nonmonetary kind. In that case, the demand for dollar money would scarcely fall at all.

This effect, if it is significant, would show up statistically as a reduction in the velocity of circulation of money in Germany and a rise in velocity in the United States. But, such effects, if any, seem to be too small to be separated out from other factors influencing velocity in the two countries in the period under review. We are therefore unable to say whether the flight from the dollar in the early 1970s had any effect at all on the world price level.

## DID EURODOLLARS CAUSE WORLD INFLATION?

The rapid buildup of dollar deposits in banks outside the United States (Eurodollars) coincided with the period of accelerating world money growth. This coincidence has led knowledgeable people to see the growth of Eurodollars and other Eurocurrencies as an important cause of world inflation—one, moreover, which is thought to be autonomous, in the sense that it depends simply on the demand for Eurocurrency credit and not on the decisions of monetary authorities.[7] We doubt this line of reasoning. Properly measured, Eurocurrency deposits do not add enough to the world money stock to account for what happened to prices. Moreover, the supply of Eurodollars and other Eurocurrencies does not appear to be autonomous, since it is influenced by the same national monetary policies that control the growth of the domestic stocks of the same currencies.

A recent, authoritative article by Helmut Mayer of the Bank for International Settlements (BIS) takes issue with the view that Eurocurrency deposits constitute a large addition to the world money supply. He points out that about three quarters of net Eurocurrency deposits as estimated by the BIS are already counted, directly or indirectly, in domestic monetary aggregates and are therefore already included in measures of the world money stock that exclude Eurocurrencies. Moreover, most Eurocurrency deposits are akin to certificates of deposit (CDs) rather than to demand or time deposits. Thus, if Eurocurrencies are to be added to a world money aggregate, the aggregate should be a broad one such as M4, which in the United States includes CDs, rather than M1 or M2, which do not. If these two qualifications are taken into account, the statistical importance of Eurocurrencies as an element in world money is greatly reduced. As Mayer concludes, "On balance, and contrary to the assumptions in the [Laffer study]. . . . hardly any addition would have to be made to the narrowly defined world money stock (M1); what would have to be added to the other world monetary aggregates (M2, M3, M4, etc.) might be about 25 percent of the BIS net size estimate, about $50 billion at present. Expressed as a precentage of relatively liquid world financial assets, this would hardly amount to more than 2 or 3 percent."[8]

Nor can the supply of Eurocurrencies be considered autonomous in the sense of being outside the control of national monetary authorities. Because there are no legal reserve requirements on dollar deposits in banks outside the United States, competition to acquire dollar deposits has driven some U.S. dollar banking offshore. But, the foreign situs of the depositories and the absence of legal reserve requirements does not mean that the Eurodollar market is uncontrolled; it only means that the control—by the U.S. Federal Reserve through its open market operations—is less obvious and direct than in the case of dollar deposits in banks in the United States.

Banks outside the United States which accept dollar deposits and extend dollar loans do so with regard to the state of their liquidity in dollars. Their dollar loans and deposits will bear, over time, a certain relationship to their working

7 See, e.g., A. Laffer, "Global Money Growth and Inflation," *The Wall Street Journal*, September 25, 1975.

8 Helmut Mayer, "The BIS Concept of the Eurocurrency Market," *Euromoney* (May 1976), p. 66.

balances (demand or short-term time deposits) held in banks in the United States, and their confirmed lines of short-term credit with their correspondent banks in the United States. This means that, in principle, the Eurodollar market should grow along with the U.S. monetary base. For the U.S. banks that provide dollar liquidity to banks in the Eurodollar market are restricted in their ability to do so by the growth of their own reserves. In fact, Eurodollar deposits seem to grow at a fairly constant trend rate plus an amount that is dictated by the availability of U.S. base money—in other words, by U.S. monetary policy.[9]

## DIFFERENCES IN RATES OF MONEY GROWTH

The hypothesis that U.S. monetary policy played the major part in the drama of world inflation has also been challenged on the ground that money growth rates in the other industrial countries during the period 1968–75 were a good deal higher than in the United States.[10] This challenge raises the question whether the diversity of money growth rates among the industrial countries can be explained by our hypothesis.

According to theory, as long as exchange rates are fixed or stabilized, monetary conditions should be similar and price levels approximately equal in all the countries participating in the system. In the long run, then, under a dollar standard, U.S. monetary conditions should determine conditions in other countries, but this does not imply that rates of monetary expansion should be equal. Since the demand for money varies with real income, among other factors, and since these factors differ widely among countries, the model suggests that money growth rates should differ in proportion as such demand factors differ. To repeat, it is monetary *conditions*—not money growth rates—that should be similar in a fixed exchange-rate system.

In the period 1966–69, the annual rate of growth of the narrowly defined money supply (M1) in five large industrial countries was 3.7 percentage points higher than in the United States. In the period 1970–73, the difference widened to

---

9 Evidence in support of this conclusion, based on an econometric model, is summarized in "A Fast-Growing Eurochild and its U.S. Parent," Citibank *Money International* (July-August 1975). There were, of course, periods when the growth of the Eurodollar stock was faster or slower than the rate predicted by this model. This was the case, for example, in 1968–69. But, this episode highlights the unity of the domestic and Eurodollar markets by showing how easy it is for depositors to substitute one for the other. In 1968–69, Federal Reserve Regulation Q interest-rate ceilings were below current U.S. market interest rates, so American banks and depositors had a strong incentive to transfer dollar deposits to their overseas branches, where higher rates of interest could be paid. Otherwise, U.S. banks would have lost business to non-U.S. Eurobanks. As a result, there was substantial "disintermediation" from the domestic dollar market to the Eurodollar market. Disintermediation was reversed later, when the Regulation Q ceilings were lifted, and for a time the growth of the Eurodollar market fell below the rate predicted by the model. In other words, changes in the regulatory environment altered the distribution of a given stock of dollar deposits as between the domestic market and the Eurodollar market, without greatly affecting the total volume of the world's stock of dollars. And, this world stock of dollars seems, itself, to be determined by the actions of the Federal Reserve system through its control of the quantity of dollar reserves available to the world banking system.

10 See, e.g., Heller, "International Reserves," and Laffer, "Global Money Growth."

9.8 percentage points. If these differences are adjusted to take into account the fact that the trend growth of real income in the other five countries was a good deal higher than in the United States, the differences narrow to 2.3 percentage points in 1966–69 and 4.8 percentage points in 1970–72.[11] (A correction should also be made for other factors, such as velocity trends, influencing the demand for money; unfortunately, these cannot be as reliably measured as differences in real income growth rates.) In sum, the large observed differences in money growth rates do not imply nearly as much difference in monetary conditions, nor as much national autonomy in creating those conditions, as might at first appear.

---

11 The five countries are Canada, Japan, Britain, France, and Germany. Money (M1) and real income (real GNP) data were taken from Appendix Tables A-2 and A-3. The money figures used are 3-quarter moving averages. For purposes of the comparison, they were converted into dollars at exchange rates actually prevailing during the periods. The real GNP figures are 12-quarter moving averages. A 12-quarter moving average was used for real growth, consistent with the generally accepted view that the demand for money is more closely related to average income over a considerable period of time (i.e., "expected" or "permanent" income) than to income in the current period. Converting the five other countries' money supplies into dollars at prevailing exchange rates has the effect of netting out changes in domestic monetary conditions that had been fully reflected in exchange-rate movements. This permits us to abstract from changes in monetary conditions that are long term in character, because they have been validated, so to speak, by an exchange-rate change.

# The Varieties of Inflationary Experience 5

If U.S. monetary policy was the most important factor in the inflationary experience of the industrial countries in the late 1960s and early 1970s, how is the diversity of their inflations to be explained in a manner which is consistent with our model of international inflation under the dollar standard? It might seem that the model requires that rates of inflation be more or less equal. If so, the large differences in inflation rates that actually occurred would contradict the model. However, this implication is not justified, either analytically or empirically.

In the first place, the model describes a long-run equilibrium—a condition that will be reached when an adjustment process that lasts at least two years is complete. It does not imply that, in shorter periods, monetary conditions in other countries will stay in line with those in the United States. In the short run, monetary conditions in the several countries may get out of line with each other, even though exchange rates remain unchanged, due to short-run differences in domestic monetary policies. For the transmission mechanism operates with a lag of some two years' duration, as was noted earlier. Accordingly, one would expect that in any given period, measured rates of inflation would differ between the United States and other industrial countries, owing to chance divergences in domestic monetary policies, even if exchange rates remained fixed or stable. Temporary divergence of inflation rates would be particularly likely in a period like that of the late sixties and early seventies, in which monetary policies in the United States and the other industrial countries were subject to large changes.

Moreover, there may be differences in rates of inflation among the industrial countries even in the long run, to the extent that exchange rates change. A floating exchange rate will equilibrate the supply of and the demand for a country's currency in the exchange market, so that no net inflow (or outflow) of funds will occur. Therefore, the link between the country's monetary base and monetary conditions in the United States is severed. Likewise, a floating exchange rate breaks the link between foreign and domestic prices, and thus allows the domestic price level to be determined by domestic monetary policy and the local demand for money alone. Also, any country that chooses to revalue its currency upward against the dollar can, to the extent of the adjustment, keep its price level below that of the United States, provided it also follows a less expansive domestic monetary policy than the United States. Conversely, any country that is willing to let its currency depreciate against the dollar, can have a higher rate of inflation than the United States, provided it also follows a more expansive domestic monetary policy than the United States.

Finally, differences of inflation among countries in any given period may be explained by the existence of a disequilibrium among their price levels at the start of the period. Or, it might reflect a devaluation of one country's exchange rate that caused it to be undervalued relative to other currencies at the beginning of the

**TABLE 5-1**

**Increases in Consumer Prices in Seven Industrial Countries: 1960-75 (in percent)**

| Country | 1960:IQ - 1967:IVQ | | 1968:IQ - 1973:IVQ | | 1968:IQ - 1975:IVQ | |
|---|---|---|---|---|---|---|
| | (1) | (2) Difference from U.S. | (3) | (4) Difference from U.S. | (5) | (6) Difference from U.S. |
| U.S. | 15.0% | | 34.2% | | 61.5% | |
| Canada | 18.8 | 3.8% | 31.4 | - 2.8% | 62.0 | 0.5% |
| France | 30.1 | 15.1 | 46.7 | 15.3 | 85.1 | 23.6 |
| Germany | 21.7 | 6.7 | 31.0 | - 3.2 | 47.2 | -14.3 |
| Italy | 35.7 | 20.7 | 38.1 | 3.9 | 91.9 | 30.4 |
| Japan (actual) | 49.0 | 34.0 | 51.6 | 17.4 | 106.2 | 44.7 |
| Japan (adjusted) | – | – | 36.6 | 2.4 | 85.8 | 24.3 |
| U.K. | 29.1 | 14.1 | 53.2 | 19.0 | 126.8 | 65.3 |

Note: Columns (1), (3) and (5) show the percentage increase in consumer price indices in the three periods indicated. Columns (2), (4) and (6) show the differences in percentage points between the increase in the U.S. index and the increase in the other countries' indices, in the same three periods. A positive figure indicates that the other country's inflation was greater than the U.S.'s inflation. The Japan (adjusted) figures are the Japan (actual) data adjusted in the manner and for the reasons set forth on pages 29-30 of the text. No adjustment to the Japan (actual) data was made for the 1960-67 period, because this period largely coincides with the period from which the adjustment was estimated. See page 30, note 3.

Source: Appendix Table A-1.

period. In this case, the higher external price level would exert upward pressure, via competition and arbitrage, on the devaluing country's price level until price-level parity (purchasing-power parity) was restored. During the period of adjustment, the devaluing country's measured rate of inflation would be higher than that of other countries.

These general considerations explain why the observed diversity of inflation among industrial countries is not inconsistent with the view that U.S. monetary policy was the major factor determining the general acceleration of world inflation from the mid-1960s on.

Table 5-1 compares the inflationary experience of the seven principal industrial countries in three periods in terms of consumer prices. The first period, 1960–67, is one of relatively low inflation; the second and third periods bracket the Great Inflation. Further information is given in Chart 5-1, which compares the relative purchasing power of the seven currencies, measured in terms of U.S. dollars rather than local currencies. Changes in the respective price levels have been corrected for changes in exchange rates, so that the chart shows changes in the respective purchasing powers of the currencies. The horizontal line in the chart represents the U.S. price level; the other lines represent the price levels of the other six countries, expressed in dollars at current rates of exchange.

## THE FIRST PERIOD

From 1960 to 1967, inflation in all the European countries was higher than in the United States. In part, this was a reflection of the slowdown of inflation in the United States in the early 1960s, as compared with the 1950s. It was probably due to the unusually deep U.S. recession of 1957–58, followed by another recession in 1960–61, which lowered the rate of inflation and price expectations in the United States well below that prevailing in the 1950s. In Europe, these two recessions were much milder.

European monetary and exchange-rate policies also contributed to higher inflation there. In Britain, for instance, monetary conditions in this period were more expansive than in the United States. This is suggested by the rise in the Bank of England's domestic assets (see Chart 6-4 in the next chapter), along with the almost continuous deficit in Britain's overall balance of payments. (The cumulative deficit in the period 1960–67 was nearly £ 3.5 billion.) While the excess supply of money generated by an expansive monetary policy was partly dissipated via the balance of payments, enough remained at home to help raise the British price level relative to the U.S. price level.

In the case of France, the franc's undervaluation at the start of the period, rather than domestic monetary policy, probably accounts for most of the difference in inflation between France and the United States. The 16 percent devaluation of the franc in 1959 was widely thought to be excessive at the time, and Chart 5-1 lends support to this view. This evidence, along with the fact that the domestic assets of the Bank of France grew only a little in the period, and that France's overall balance of payments registered a substantial surplus from 1959 through 1967, suggests that the 1959 devaluation was the main domestic factor contributing to France's higher inflation. Italy's relatively high inflation rate in the same period may also reflect an initial undervaluation of the lira (see Chart 5-1). But, in Italy's case, domestic monetary policy was expansive, and the rise in the Italian price level in this period was financed mainly by domestic credit expansion rather than via a payments surplus as was the case in France.

Among the principal industrial countries, Japan's high measured inflation in the 1960–67 period is the most difficult to explain. The balance of Japan's international payments in this period—the overall balance was on average in equilibrium—suggests that monetary conditions in Japan were no more expansive than those in the United States. Yet, consumer prices in Japan rose 34 percentage points more than in the United States (see Table 5-1, Column 2). The explanation

**CHART 5-1**

**Purchasing Power of Six Currencies Relative to the U.S. Dollar**

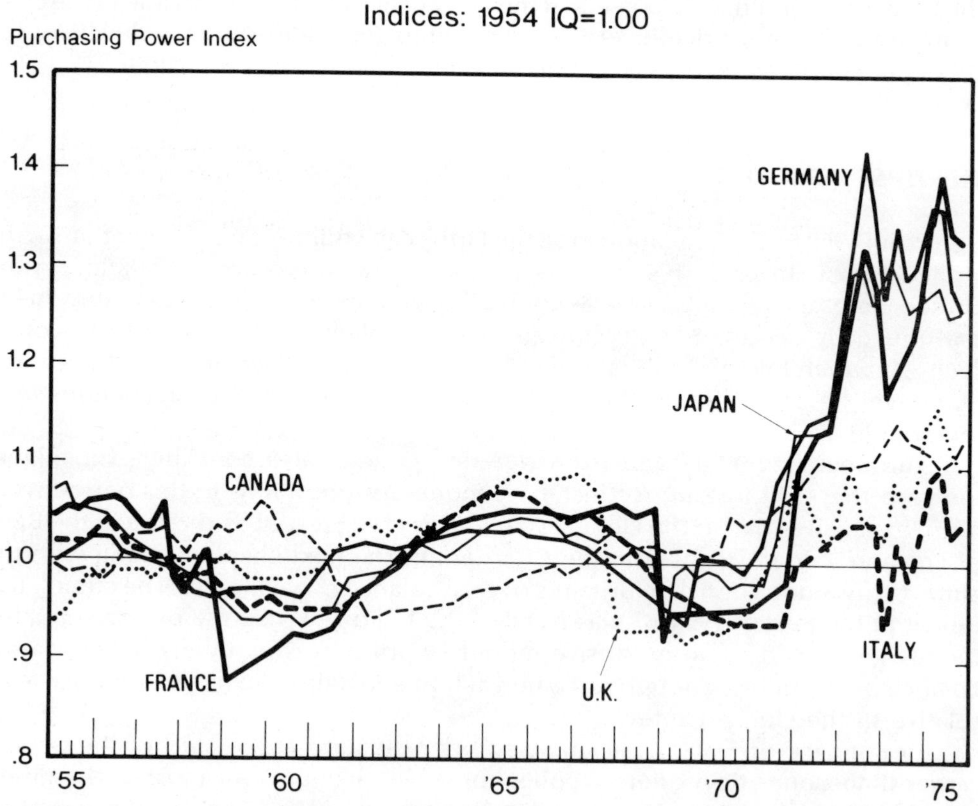


Note: When a country's purchasing power index is one, that country's consumer prices expressed in dollars using the current exchange rate are presumed to be equal to those in the United States. When the index is greater than one, that country's prices expressed in dollars using the current exchange rate are higher than in the United States. When the index is less than one, that country's prices are lower than those in the United States.

Source: Appendix Tables.

probably lies not in a difference in monetary conditions but in a problem of measurement. The apparently higher rate of inflation in Japan reflects the rapid transition of Japan during the 1960s from a semi-industrial to a highly industrialized country. It reflects not a difference of monetary conditions but a change in the quality of some consumer goods and services.[1] It may also reflect a rise in the relative prices of some Japanese consumer goods, which the consumer price index records as if there were a rise in the absolute price level.[2]

## THE GREAT INFLATION PERIOD

As monetary expansion and inflation accelerated in the United States and the other industrial countries after 1967, some differences in rates of inflation persisted, but they were dwarfed by the overall speedup in money growth and price inflation common to the countries as a group. At the beginning of the 1968–75 period, large devaluations of the pound (in November 1967) and the French franc (in August 1969) contributed along with high rates of domestic credit expansion to higher inflation in these two countries than in the United States. In France, the 1968 student uprising and general strike led to a burst of domestic credit expansion, followed by devaluation. Rapid credit expansion was required to avoid the wide-

---

1 Studies by a number of economists have shown that as an economy grows, its price level, measured by a consumer price index, tends to rise continuously, even though the exchange rate remains fixed. The theoretical explanation of this phenomenon is that, as development proceeds, the quality of domestically produced, nontraded goods and services rises. When no correction is made for quality change, goods prices appear to rise although prices of quality-adjusted units are actually constant. The overall consumer price index will increase not as a result of inflationary pressures but as a consequence of economic growth. These characteristics of a consumer price index are relevant in all countries at all stages of economic development. But, they have a large differential effect among countries when, like Japan and the United States, the countries are at different stages of development and their economies grow at very different rates.

See M. de Vries, "Exchange Depreciation in Developing Countries," *International Monetary Fund Staff Papers,* Vol. 15, No. 3 (1968), pp. 560–577; B. Balassa, "The Purchasing-Power Parity Doctrine: A Reappraisal," *Journal of Political Economy,* Vol. 72, No. 6 (December 1964), pp. 584–596; P. David, "Just How Misleading Are Official Exchange Rate Conversions," *The Economic Journal,* Vol. 82, No. 327 (September 1972), pp. 979–990. Also, M. Gilbert and I. Kravis, *An International Comparison of National Products and the Purchasing Power of Currencies* (Paris: Organization for European Economic Co-operation, 1954); Gilbert and Associates, *Comparative National Products and Price Levels: A Study of Western Europe and the United States* (Paris: Organization for European Economic Co-operation, 1958); I. Kravis et al., *A System of International Comparisons of Gross Product and Purchasing Power* (Baltimore: The Johns Hopkins University Press, 1975).

2 A second possible source of upward bias in the Japanese consumer price index relative to the U.S. index is the Japanese index's heavier weighting with labor-intensive services and agricultural goods, whose relative prices tend to rise along with wages. Wages in Japan normally rise faster than U.S. wages, due to the Japanese economy's higher growth rate. Thus, the heavier weighting of labor-intensive items in the Japanese index tends to bias it upward *vis à vis* the U.S. index. This is true, at any rate, unless the weights in the Japanese index are adjusted promptly to reflect the changing proportions in which goods and services are actually consumed. This has apparently not been consistently done. As a result, some part of the apparent difference in Japanese and U.S. inflation during the postwar period, as measured by consumer price indexes, may be due to this measurement problem. See H. Patrick and H. Rosovsky, "Japan's Economic Performance: An Overview," in Patrick and Rosovsky, eds., *Asia's New Giant: How the Japanese Economy Works* (Washington, 1976), pp. 25–27.

spread financial pressure on firms and the unemployment that would otherwise have resulted from the massive general increase of wages that settled the strike. The ensuing pressure on the exchange rate of the franc brought on the 1969 devaluation.

Except in these two countries, the divergences in inflation rates among the seven countries were smaller in the 1968–73 period than they had been in the earlier period (see Table 5-1, Column 4). Indeed, if the Japanese consumer price index is adjusted to allow for the measurement problems discussed above,[3] the inflations in the principal industrial countries, with the exception of Britain and France, hardly differed in the period 1968 through 1973—and this despite the fact that in all the countries, the average annual rate of inflation was more than double that of the 1960–67 period. In the first phase of the Great Inflation, then, it indeed seems that U.S. monetary policy called the tune of world inflation.

From 1972 on, however, although inflation continued to accelerate everywhere, monetary policies and rates of inflation increasingly diverged (see Table 5-1, Column 6). Thus, Germany maintained a tight grip on domestic credit expansion and allowed the mark to rise against the dollar, and German inflation fell well below U.S. inflation. In Britain, Italy and Japan, large fiscal deficits were "monetized" by the central bank, leading to an upturn in inflation steeper than in the United States. The British, Italian and Japanese balances of payments fell into deficit and these countries' currencies depreciated against the dollar. Canada was the only country where monetary conditions and the pace of inflation failed to diverge from that of the United States in the Great Inflation's final phase.

---

3 To estimate the true inflation differential between Japan and the United States, we adjusted the Japanese consumer price index by removing the trend component in the ratio of Japanese prices to U.S. prices as calculated over the period of fixed exchange rates—1955 to 1970. The trend was calculated by regressing the log of this ratio on time. The trend so determined was statistically significant and largely independent of the time period specified. It indicated an annual noninflationary rise of the Japanese consumer price index relative to the U.S. index of about 2.3 percent per year.

# The Political Economy of World Inflation 6

These comparisons of monetary conditions in the industrial countries bring us to the final and most difficult question—why did governments and central banks choose the monetary and exchange-rate policies that led to these untoward results? The question takes us into the realm of political economy and economic history—disciplines in which we claim no special competence. What follows should therefore be taken as particularly tentative and unavoidably partial. We hope, nevertheless, that it will shed some light on the question why the inflationary process in the period 1968–75 was allowed to run out of control.

## THE UNITED STATES

Considering the major role assigned to U.S. monetary conditions in our story of the Great Inflation, the first task is to explain the U.S. inflation itself. In strictly economic terms, there is not much to add to what has been said already; the more or less continuous accleration of U.S. inflation from the early 1960s through 1974 was a consequence of the acceleration of U.S. money growth.

In the years 1960–65, the narrowly defined U.S. money stock (M1) grew at an average annual rate of about 3 percent. From 1965 to 1970, money growth accelerated to 5 percent per annum, despite two periods of monetary restraint in 1966 and again in 1969, which brought on, respectively, the mini-recession of 1967 and the 1970 slump. Then money growth accelerated still more, averaging about 7 percent per annum in the three years 1971–73. It slowed again to an average of 4.7 percent in 1974–75 (see Chart 6-1). Over the period we have called the Great Inflation—first quarter 1968–fourth quarter 1975—the U.S. money stock (M1) grew 56 percent and U.S. consumer prices rose 62 percent. It appears that the U.S. price level normally rises over extended periods a little more slowly than the narrowly defined money stock.[1] If so, the U.S. price level in fourth quarter 1975 was a little lower than it should have been, given the antecedent rise in M1—no doubt because, by the end of 1975, the U.S. price level had not yet adjusted fully to the money growth that had occurred up to that time.

A bit more difficult to explain than the magnitude of the cumulative rise in prices is the timing of price increases, and particularly the steep run up in prices in 1974, when consumer prices in the United States rose 11 percent, year-over-year. Given that U.S. money growth (M1) never exceeded 7-8 percent per annum on a sustained basis, the annual rate of inflation in 1974 is surprisingly high. The

1 This presupposes that the trend growth in velocity of M1 is largely offset by the trend growth of the demand for money, due to the growth of real income, so that the equilibrium rate of inflation is not much below the average growth of M1 over an extended period.

**CHART 6-1**

**The U.S. Money Stock**

**Currency in circulation plus demand deposits of the commercial banking system (M1)**

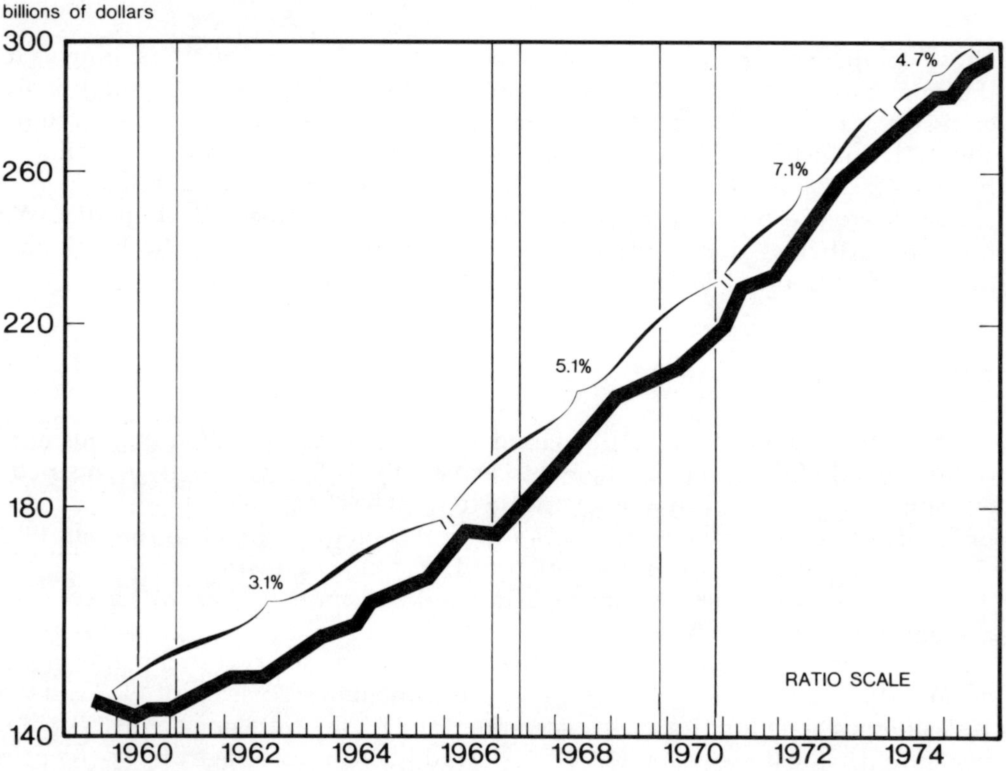


Source: Appendix Tables.

explanation is probably to be found in a number of nonmonetary causes, including the oil price increases and the other supply factors discussed above. Another factor was U.S. price controls. Imposed in August 1971 and lifted in the second half of 1973, price controls suppressed some of the increase in prices that would otherwise have occurred during the control period and shifted it forward into the latter part of 1973 and 1974.[2]

The progressive devaluation of the dollar over the period 1971–73 against the continental European currencies and the Japanese yen may also have contributed to U.S. inflation, although the importance of this factor has probably been exaggerated. The U.S. economy is larger than the combined economies of the countries

2 See, e.g., A. Burger, "The Current Inflation: The United States Experience," Federal Reserve Bank of St. Louis *Review* (September 1974), p. 16.

whose currencies appreciated markedly against the dollar. Accordingly, more than half the effect on prices of the change in currency values would show up as a temporarily lower rate of inflation in these other countries and less than half as a temporarily higher rate of inflation in the United States. Moreover, the dollar did not depreciate against the Canadian dollar or against many of the Latin American and Asian currencies. For these reasons, the effect of the dollar's devaluation on the U.S. price level could hardly have been large.

Two political and ideological changes were critical in explaining U.S. monetary expansion. One was a marked shift in the spirit of U.S. domestic economic management. With the inauguration of President Kennedy in 1961, U.S. domestic economic policy took on an activist, expansionist tone in contrast to the more passive, cautious policies of the Eisenhower years. This spirit continued to characterize U.S. fiscal and monetary management through the two Johnson Administrations and the first Nixon Administration (1968–72). The second and closely related change was rising federal deficits, due not only to the fiscal activism and ideological bent of the Kennedy and Johnson Administrations but also to the war in Vietnam. Rising deficits, "monetized" in substantial part by Federal Reserve purchases of government debt, were a major cause of the accelerating rise in the U.S. money stock.[3]

Three decisions shaped the course of U.S. monetary policy in the period under review. The first was the Johnson Administration's decision, announced in July 1965, to provide all-out support to the government of South Vietnam. As a consequence of this commitment and of the Administration's adoption of a series of ambitious social programs under the label of the Great Society, federal expenditures, which had risen by about 6 percent a year from 1957 to 1965, rose at an annual rate of nearly 15 percent for the following three years. A federal tax increase, mooted in 1965, was delayed until 1968. A burst of money growth ensued that lasted well into 1966, as the Federal Reserve pumped reserves into the banking system in an effort to slow the rise of interest rates caused by heavy government borrowing in the face of strong private demand for credit.[4]

In mid-1966, as the economy boomed and prices accelerated, the Federal Reserve tightened up. The result was a "credit crunch"—a three-way collision between public and private credit demands and tight money. Money growth slowed and the economy slid down into the mini-recession of 1967. Inflation slowed promptly, as the rate of inflation expected by the public was still under the sway of the nearly stable price level of the early 1960s and below the current rate of inflation. But, the authorities were more impressed with the turmoil in the financial

---

3 As Darryl R. Francis, President of the Federal Reserve Bank of St. Louis, put it in May 1974, "In the decade 1952 until the latter part of 1961, the net Government debt rose by a total of $22 billion. Of that amount, the Federal Reserve, through its open market operations, 'monetized' about $5 billion. The relatively slow growth of Government debt and debt owned by the Federal Reserve . . . produced a rise of our money stock of less than 2 percent per year. This is why prices rose so slowly through the 1950s and into the early 1960s. . . . [I]n the past twelve years [1962–74], the Federal Reserve has acquired over one-half of the $100 billion increase in our net national debt, contributing to almost doubling of our money supply. . . . In my view, the successive upward ratcheting in the average growth rate of the money stock has been the primary cause of the acceleration in the average rate of inflation." Federal Reserve Bank of St. Louis *Review* (May 1974), pp. 6–7.

4 A.J. Meigs, *Money Matters* (New York, 1972), p. 45.

markets than with their success in slowing inflation. In 1967, the Federal Reserve again turned strongly expansive and the money supply ballooned.

The decision to expand money rapidly in 1967 and to continue that policy in 1968 was the second major turning point in the drama of U.S. inflation. Again, the underlying reasons were fiscal, although this time there was a new twist. The Federal Reserve and the Administration were fearful that the 10 percent income tax surcharge expected to be enacted in 1968 would abort the recovery from the 1967 slowdown. These misplaced fears of "fiscal overkill," as it was called at the time, along with the continuing pressure to accommodate the government's large borrowing requirement, caused the Federal Reserve to expand the monetary base at historically high rates through 1968. The payoff was a sharp upturn in inflation, to 5½ percent in 1969 and almost 6 percent in 1970.

Late in 1968, the monetary authorities renewed the fight against inflation, and tightened further in 1969 as the first Nixon Administration took office. The new Administration's economic watchword was "gradualism," a term intended to suggest a policy of slowing inflation down gradually, mainly by moderate monetary restraint, and thus hopefully avoiding a severe impact on business activity and employment. But, gradualism, as James Meigs later wrote, was "[n]ot for the Fed. . . . [T]he System was just recovering from its embarrassing reaction to the fears of 'fiscal overkill' that seized Washington when the [tax surcharge] of 1968 was passed. . . . Some of them were troubled by the thought that if they had stuck to their guns a little longer in 1966 . . . they could have beat back inflation before it became so well entrenched."[5] Also, the Federal budget swung into surplus in 1968, and this gave the Federal Reserve a freer hand to tighten money. As a result, money growth in the second half of 1969 slowed to a crawl, and the economy plunged into recession. Unlike the 1967 experience, however, the impact of monetary restraint on inflation was disappointing. By 1970, the public's expectations of inflation had been ratcheted up by the higher pace of inflation prevailing since 1965, and inflation showed no sign of moderating.

It was this fundamental change in the economic environment that underlay the third and most fateful shift of U.S. monetary policy toward expansion. Early in 1970 and with greater emphasis in 1971, the Federal Reserve turned expansive again and maintained that posture more or less consistently through 1972. This policy was a response to business conditions and rising unemployment, as the Federal Reserve, along with the Administration, became increasingly concerned about the sluggishness of the recovery from the 1970 recession. The weakness of the recovery was due essentially to the momentum of inflationary expectations. Rising prices, impelled by expectations of continuing inflation at 4 to 5 percent per annum, absorbed a large part of the initial increase in nominal incomes resulting from the monetary stimulus, limiting the response of real output and employment. As recovery continued to lag and the presidential election of 1972 came closer, the Administration pushed harder for a more expansive monetary policy—and with increasing effect.[6]

---

5 Ibid., p. 67.

6 Sherman Maisel, a member of the Federal Reserve Board at the time, tells the story of the Nixon Administration's influence on monetary policy in 1972 in his book, *Managing the Dollar* (New York, 1973), p. 278.

Throughout this whole period, U.S. monetary policymakers acted as though subject to no serious international constraints.[7] Except in 1966 and in 1969, when U.S. monetary policy was temporarily restrictive, the U.S. balance of payments was on a strongly deteriorating trend from 1965 to 1973, as monetary theory suggests it should have been. This was particularly true in 1971–72, when the rapidly growing outflow of funds from the United States due to accelerated monetary expansion was swollen by large speculative movements. For the exchange markets judged—correctly—that this turn to monetary expansion spelled *finis* for the dollar's exchange rate *vis à vis* other principal currencies. But, the link between monetary expansion in the United States, the U.S. balance-of-payments deficit, and the expansion of foreign money stocks and inflation abroad was not generally understood in the United States during the critical period of U.S. money expansion from 1967 to 1973. The efforts of European officials to suggest a connection were offically dismissed as attempts to blame the United States for the shortcomings of European fiscal and monetary management.[8]

The crucial errors of U.S. economic management were the Federal Reserve's attempt to kill inflation with one blow in 1969, followed by the Fed's and the Administration's highly expansive policy in 1971 and 1972. If "gradualism" had prevailed in 1969, or if monetary expansion had been less rapid in the aftermath of the 1970 recession, the world inflation of the 1970s would not have reached the dimensions that have gained it a large and dubious place in the economic history of the 20th century.

---

7 As Sherman Maisel noted, "I estimate that international considerations caused a change in the actual target of the FOMC [Federal Reserve Open Market Committee] during the period I served on the Fed [1965–72], from what it would have been on purely domestic grounds in only eight out of more than one hundred directives. . . . The percentage of Board policy decisions affected [by balance-of-payments or other international considerations] was probably about the same." Ibid., p. 221.

8 In the late 1960s, the usual explanation of the U.S. balance-of-payments problem was that the dollar was overvalued. This explanation was based on a nonmonetary approach to the balance of payments. The overall payments deficit was considered to be simply the sum of the deficits on capital and current account—the former being determined by relative U.S. and foreign prices, the exchange rate and the level of income; the latter being determined by interest differentials. U.S. policy options were accordingly considered to be limited to increasing U.S. competitiveness through devaluation, restraining imports by slowing the U.S. economy, increasing U.S. interest rates relative to those overseas by monetary restraint, and imposing direct controls on particular items of the U.S. balance of payments. Controls on capital flows were imposed by the U.S. authorities in the 1960s, when the Voluntary Foreign Credit Restraint and Overseas Foreign Direct Investment programs and the Interest Equalization Tax were instituted. When these failed to bring the deficit under control, devaluation became the chosen remedy, monetary restraint having been ruled out on domestic grounds.

See, e.g., "Exchange Rate Adjustment," *Factors Affecting the United States Balance of Payments,* Joint Economic Committee, 87th Congress, 2nd Session (Washington, 1962), pp. 289–304, where Hendrick Houthakker, later a member of the Council of Economic Advisors, explained how the U.S. dollar was overvalued. The policy options for curing the deficit as they were seen at the time were fully elaborated by John E. Floyd in "The Overvaluation of the Dollar: A Note on the International Price Mechanism," *American Economic Review,* Vol. 55, No. 1 (March 1965), pp. 95–107; in Martin J. Prachowny, *A Structural Model of the U.S. Balance of Payments* (Amsterdam: North Holland Publishing Company, 1969); and in Peter B. Kenen, "Short-term Capital Movements and the U.S. Balance of Payments," *Hearings Before the Joint Economic Committee,* 88th Congress, 1st Session (Washington, D.C., 1963), pp. 153–191.

## GERMANY

Of the principal industrial countries, Germany was most successful in resisting the inflationary tide flowing from the United States. This relative success stems fundamentally from political causes: in Germany, the authorities and the public gave a higher priority to price stability than was the case in the other industrial countries. This traditional German attitude was reflected institutionally in the greater political independence of the central bank and in the government's reluctance to incur large budget deficits.

More particularly, German monetary policy in the period of the Great Inflation was remarkably conservative, by international standards. Between 1968 and 1974,

### CHART 6-2

### Sources of the German Monetary Base

Note: Components are converted using current exchange rates.

Source: IMF International Financial Statistics and the Federal Reserve Bulletin.

the Bundesbank's domestic assets hardly increased, almost the entire increase in the German monetary base being contributed by a persistent surplus in the balance of payments. (See Chart 6-2.) And, when this monetary policy brought strong upward pressure on the mark-dollar exchange rate—as it was bound to do given U.S. monetary policy—the German authorities were less hesitant than their counterparts in some other countries to let their currency appreciate against the dollar, in order to weaken the link between German prices and prices abroad. The results of this policy stance are evident in Germany's lower rate of inflation (see Table 5-1 in the preceeding chapter, p. 26). The results may also be seen in Chart 6-3, which shows that from 1967 on, German money growth adjusted for changes in the trend growth rate of real GNP was on a downward trend relative to U.S. money growth similarly adjusted. The trend growth rates of GNP serve as proxies for money

**CHART 6-3**

**Differences in Monetary Conditions in Germany and the United States: 1955–75**

**German and U.S. money growth rates:**
**Actual and adjusted for trend growth rates of real GNP**

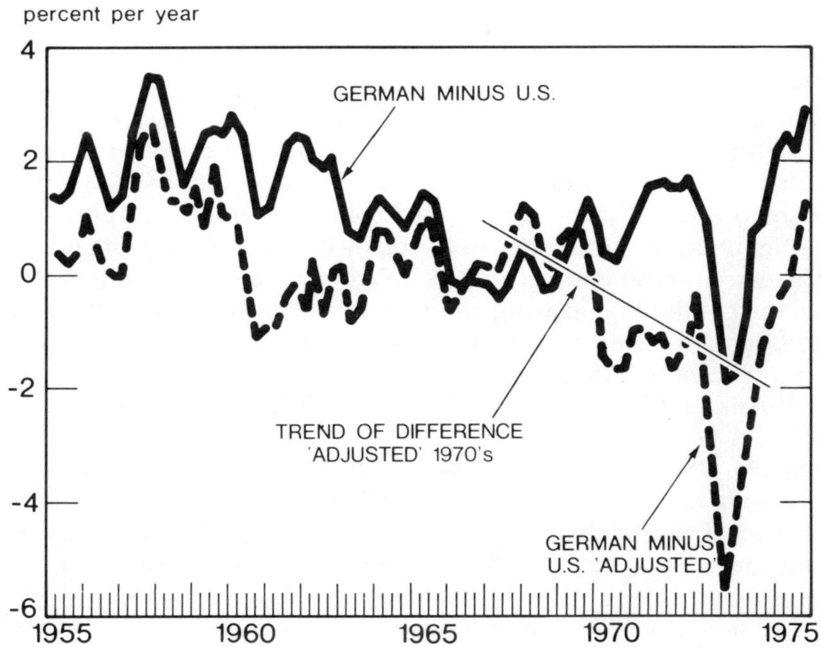


Note: Each country's money series was adjusted for differences in money demand by subtracting a 12-quarter moving average of real GNP growth from the 3-quarter moving average of money supply growth.

Source: Appendix Tables.

demand in the two countries. Quite evidently, monetary conditions in Germany were distinctly less expansive than conditions in the United States and the other main industrial countries in the period under review.

We shall begin our brief account of the German inflation with the German recession of 1967 and its aftermath. In 1965–66, with prices accelerating in the United States, inflation was accelerating in Germany too. Alarmed, the Bundesbank restricted credit sharply—indeed brutally—beginning in mid-1966. The effect of this action was compounded by the Federal Reserve's more or less simultaneous—but less drastic—move toward restraint. The German money supply slowed abruptly, and for two quarters actually fell. The result was the short, sharp recession of 1967. German prices responded strongly; inflation measured by consumer prices slowed from 3½ percent in 1966 to 1.7 percent in 1968–69, a time when inflation in the United States was running at 4½–5½ percent (see Appendix Table A-1, p. 54).

These price developments not only gave a boost to German exports, they also put the German price level temporarily somewhat below the U.S. and world price levels. Thus, with exchange rates fixed, German inflation was bound to accelerate again as German prices were pulled up to the world level. By the autumn of 1969, German wages and prices were in fact accelerating, and to the Bundesbank "it was clear that the long-feared adjustment of domestic prices and costs to the higher foreign level was fully under way."[9] With exchange rates fixed, rising inflation in Germany was the more inevitable as inflation in the United States and in the rest of the world generally was also accelerating.

From 1966 on, the Bundesbank continued to lean against the inflationary wind, following a domestic credit policy that was consistently moderate to restrictive. With the Bank's domestic assets more or less constant, the money needed to finance rising prices in Germany was provided by a continuous rise in the Bank's foreign assets (see Chart 6-2, p. 36), whose counterpart was a balance-of-payments surplus characterized by a massive trade surplus and a large capital inflow. The central bank professed surprise that the trade and payments surplus should continue despite booming conditions in Germany in 1968–69, pointing to "the failure of the balance of trade and services to react 'normally,' by a tendency towards deficit, to the continuing upswing and increasing tensions at home."[10] But, given the Bundesbank's conservative domestic credit policy, the earlier decline in German prices relative to U.S. prices, and the Federal Reserve's expansive policy in 1968 and the first half of 1969, both the trade surplus and the capital inflow were inevitable.

Inevitable, too, were the expectations engendered by this state of affairs that the mark would be revalued. So it happened that the year 1969 was punctuated by a series of speculative attacks on the mark-dollar rate, culminating in a brief period of floating and then an upward adjustment of parity in October 1969. This move, forced by currency speculation, was immediately aimed at bringing speculation to an end. But, it also reflected the reasoned judgment of the Bundesbank and the government that revaluation was the best way to cope with inflation in Germany.

---

9 Deutsche Bundesbank, Annual Report for the Year 1969, p. 7.

10 Ibid., p. 8.

According to the Bundesbank, "The revaluation of the Deutsche Mark [in 1969] was designed to check, as quickly and as lastingly as possible, internal economic activity and the domestic price rise."[11]

While the 1969 revaluation undoubtedly served the purpose of making Germany's inflation lower than it would otherwise have been, it conspicuously failed to convince the markets—except briefly—that the new mark-dollar parity would hold. Given U.S. and German monetary policies, this is hardly surprising. As already noted, early in 1970, the Federal Reserve, after a brief period of restraint in 1969, had turned expansive again and became still more so in 1971, while German monetary policy, which had also been tight in 1969, remained so throughout 1970.[12] The result was to enlarge Germany's balance-of-payments surplus and to renew the speculative pressure on the mark-dollar rate. The effort to hold domestic money growth down was also frustrated. Reflecting the speedup of U.S. money growth in 1970, Germany's money supply grew twice as strongly in 1970 as in 1969. "The main reason for this was not domestic credit expansion, which declined slightly compared with [1969], but the unusually sharp rise in the net external assets of the banking system."[13] As the Bundesbank was wont to put it, it had lost control over domestic liquidity because, under a system of fixed exchange rates, its external flank was wide open.

The period between the October 1969 revaluation and the final decision to float the mark in February 1973 was one of acute frustration for the German authorities and particularly for the Bundesbank. Given the Federal Reserve's expansiveness and their own desire, for fear of inflation, to hold down domestic credit expansion, a large, continuing balance-of-payments surplus was unavoidable, with consequent strong speculative pressure on the currency. And, given their remaining—though gradually weakening—commitment to the Bretton Woods system of pegged exchanged rates, an acceleration of domestic inflation was unavoidable, too. Yet, by periodically floating the mark and revaluing it sharply in December 1971 under the Smithsonian Agreement and again the following year, and finally in February 1973 abandoning any attempt to peg the rate, Germany did succeed in reducing its subsequent rate of inflation to well below the U.S. rate. In 1974 and 1975, when U.S. consumer prices rose 11 and 9.1 percent, respectively, German consumer prices rose only 7 and 6 percent.

Given their preoccupation with inflation, it may seem surprising that the German authorities did not reach the conclusion earlier that floating was the only way of shielding the German price level from the world inflation. The reason, of course, is that inflation was not the only consideration. The authorities were also subject to pressure from industrial interests which feared the competitive consequences of a further rise in the exchange rate. As the Bundesbank put it in its 1971 report, it was constrained in its monetary and exchange-rate policies by "the steady upvaluation of the DM, which owing to the resulting deterioration of the competitive position of German trade and industry, caused the greater misgivings the

---

11 Ibid., p. 15.

12 Deutsche Bundesbank, Annual Report for the Year 1970, p. 13.

13 Ibid.

longer it persisted."[14] Nor did it help the German authorities to resolve this dilemma to know, as they did, that the U.S. government in this period believed that the amount of the dollar's devaluation accomplished in December 1971 and in the 1972 round of parity changes was insufficient to restore the large U.S. trade surplus that Treasury Secretary John Connally had announced in 1971 as a priority U.S. objective.

Yet, it would be ungenerous to fault Germans for being reluctant to face what most other countries were still less willing to accept; namely, that as long as exchange rates were pegged to the dollar, Germany was bound to share to some extent in the monetary expansion and inflation emanating from the United States. The German authorities had analyzed the problem correctly and were among the first continental European countries to accept the inevitability of floating against the dollar.

## THE UNITED KINGDOM

A dedication to full employment runs like a bright thread through British economic policy during the whole of the post-World War II period. As long as the pound's exchange rate was fixed, a large part of the excessive domestic credit creation implied by the full employment commitment spilled out via a balance-of-payments deficit, and Britain's inflation was only a little higher than inflation in the United States. But, in 1971, the British government embarked on a policy of large budget deficits and extremely rapid domestic credit expansion to speed recovery from a slump, and then in 1972 set the pound free to float—down. The result was a speedup of inflation in Britain to a pace well above that in the United States and other industrial countries.

The change of course in 1971 was a response to a conjuncture of stagnant output and rapid inflation. In 1970, inflation in Britain had speeded up to nearly 6½ percent, year-over-year, mainly as a consequence of accelerating inflation in the United States and other countries. But, the British economy was still feeling the lagged effects of tight money in the United States, in Germany and in Britain itself in 1969. In 1970, monetary conditions in Britain eased as the Federal Reserve turned expansive and the British balance of payments moved into surplus. But, the effect on spending and nominal incomes in the United Kingdom was largely absorbed by rising prices, leaving the real economy in the doldrums.

It was in these circumstances—so similar to those in the United States in the same period—that Chancellor of the Exchequer Anthony Barber brought in the first of three annual budgets, each with a larger deficit than the last. The Chancellor's budget speech of March 30, 1971 marked the turn. Although worried about inflation, he was mainly concerned about recovery:

> As far as fiscal and monetary policies are concerned, the first requirement is that they should not create any danger that demand inflation will be added to the present inflation stemming from rapidly rising costs. But the forecast which I have outlined . . . suggests that this is not the main danger at present. It is much

14 Deutsche Bundesbank, Annual Report for the Year 1971, p. 15.

> more probable that, in the absence of any change in policy, the pressure of demand would fall, and I do not believe that the fight against inflation would be aided at present by any further lowering of the pressure of demand. . . . These considerations lead one to the conclusion that the Budget should provide some addition to demand. . . . Given the current growth of incomes, there would be dangers for liquidity and employment if we sought immediately to reduce the growth of the money supply much below 3 percent per quarter.[15]

In the event, the narrowly defined money supply grew rather faster than that. In 1971, it was up 13.9 percent, year-over-year, accelerating markedly during the year as the Bank of England, attempting to accommodate rising demand for credit from both the public and private sectors, began to expand its domestic assets (see Chart 6-4). Private consumption responded to this monetary stimulus, but investment lagged. Although such a lag was a normal feature of economic recoveries in Britain, it seemed to the authorities, given the high level of unemployment, to call for greater fiscal and monetary stimulus. Furthermore, from mid-1971, inflation had begun to ease, reflecting the lagged effect of the 1969 monetary slowdown in Britain and abroad.

> I have therefore come to the conclusion [said the Chancellor in his 1972 budget speech] that a further boost in demand is required. . . . I do not believe that a stimulus to demand of the order I propose will be inimical to the fight against inflation. . . . We now have a rare opportunity to secure a sustained and faster rate of economic expansion over a considerable period of years. . . . [T]he prospects for expansion and for growing prosperity over the next five years must surely be better than they have been for a very long time.[16]

The same brave themes were repeated a year later in the Chancellor's third budget speech on March 6, 1972. By that time the British economy was clearly growing strongly, responding to the two years of highly expansive monetary conditions. But now British policymakers had lifted their sights. No longer content with stimulating an ordinary recovery, they spoke of a dash for growth—of forcing the British economy by sheer pressure of demand to raise its long-term rate of growth above what had been considered possible in the past. "We have achieved our first objective [the Chancellor said]—to lift the economy on to a path of higher growth. My aim in this Budget looking ahead over the next year or so, is to continue on that path." He recognized that the moderating trend of price and wage advances in 1971–72 had been "sharply reversed," but he counted on a program of voluntary or compulsory wage and price restraints, then under consideration, to contain the inflation.[17]

In truth, the government's "high-risk fiscal strategy," as it was dubbed by the British press, involved not so much a risk as a certainty of disastrous inflation. The 1973 budget showed a deficit three times as large as in the previous fiscal year, notwithstanding the strength of the boom and a projected steep rise in revenues.

---

15 *Hansard,* March 30, 1971, pp. 1,369–1,374.

16 *Hansard,* May 20–27, 1972, pp. 25,266–25,267.

17 *Hansard,* March 6, 1973, pp. 236–240.

**CHART 6-4**

**Sources of the British Monetary Base**

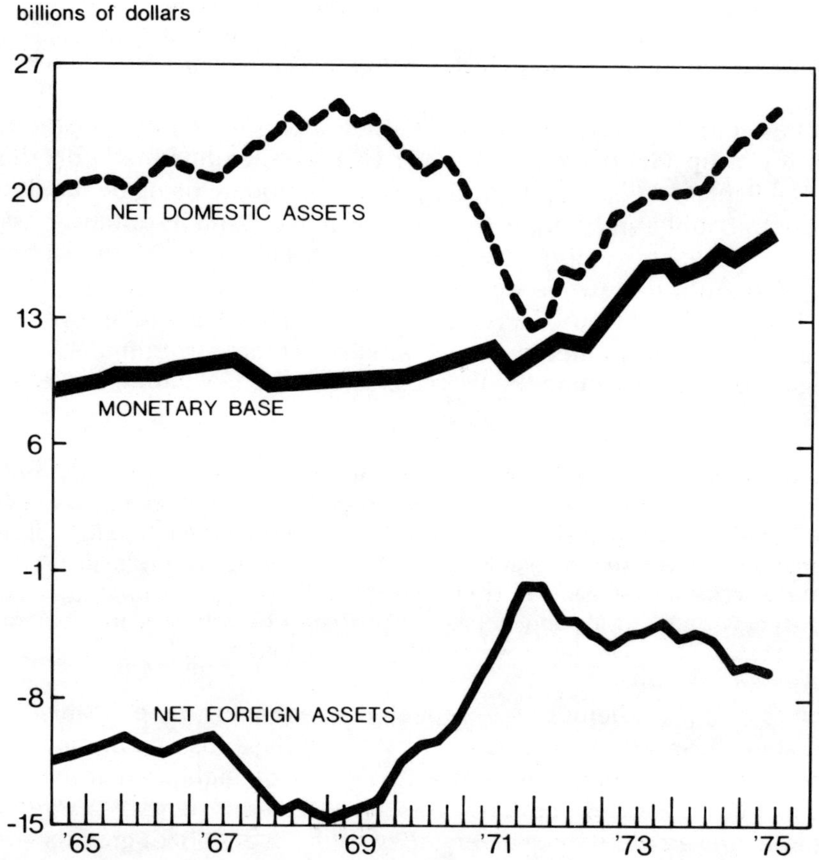


Note: Components are converted using current exchange rates.

Source: IMF International Financial Statistics and the Federal Reserve Bulletin.

In the circumstances, this necessarily implied a highly expansive posture for monetary policy. For the Treasury's heavy financing needs, the vigorous economic upturn and the resulting strong demand for credit were bound to force the Bank of England to expand credit rapidly. And so it turned out. There was an explosive rise in the Bank of England's domestic assets (see Chart 6-4), and the narrowly defined money supply ballooned. And, with the pound floating after June 1972, albeit with some continuing official support, more of the money created by the Bank of England stayed at home to raise British prices than would have been the case if the exchange rate had remained fixed. The link between British and U.S. prices was partly broken and British inflation was free to rise far above U.S. inflation, as it soon did.

The sharp acceleration of inflation in Britain to 16 percent in 1974 and 24 percent in 1975 was considerably greater than seems justified even by the high money growth rates of 1971–73. As in the United States, several nonmonetary causes were also at work. One was the price of oil, which hit Britain harder than the United States due to its greater dependence on imported oil. Another was price controls. Imposed in Britain in 1971 and tightened in 1972, controls partly suppressed inflation temporarily, pushing it ahead into 1974–75, when the controls broke down.

In sum, up to 1972, Britain's inflation was mainly of the imported variety. But, the subsequent explosive rise of British prices far above those in other industrial countries must be put down to domestic policy.

## CANADA

If inflation in Germany and unemployment in Britain have been the main preoccupations of policymakers in those countries, in Canada the authorities' main concern has been the exchange rate. For many years, the Canadian monetary authorities have usually sought to keep the Canadian dollar stable relative to the U.S. dollar. This has been true whether the exchange rate was fixed or floating.[18]

The Canadian authorities' desire to maintain a stable exchange rate with the United States springs from the openness of the Canadian economy and the integration of its financial and industrial markets with those of the United States. As Louis Rasminsky, former Governor of the Bank of Canada, put it in 1970, in an explanation of Canadian monetary policy under the new floating rate regime:

> The exchange rate is a very important price in a country that trades with the outside world on the scale that Canada does: changes in it have important effects on the level and nature of economic activity in Canada, particularly on the position of industries that export and that compete with imports. It is not possible to ignore it, even when it floats. Public financial management must continue to be concerned that the exchange rate is broadly suitable to the development of Canada's international trade, and compatible with the desired structure of our balance of payments, in particular the size of the balance on current account. It is therefore still necessary to seek a mix of fiscal and monetary policy which encourages levels of interest rates in Canada that are consistent with the exchange rate staying in a suitable range. . . . [I]f the exchange rate moves or threatens to move outside that range it will be prudent to review the mix of financial policy in Canada to see if some other mix would be more appropriate.[19]

Before June 1970, when the Canadian dollar was still pegged to the U.S. dollar, the same preoccupation was also evident. The Bank of Canada stood ready to alter its

18 The most notable exception in recent times was the 1962 devaluation of the Canadian dollar to 92½ U.S. cents. This large devaluation undervalued the Canadian dollar, and consequently raised the rate of inflation in Canada above that in the United States between 1963 and 1967.

19 Annual Report of the Governor of the Bank of Canada to the Minister of Finance (1970), pp. 9–10.

lending rates to attract or repel short-term capital flows, in order to stabilize the Canadian dollar-U.S. dollar rate.[20]

Through 1973, the Bank of Canada achieved exchange-rate stability mainly by influencing interest differentials between Canada and the United States. In 1974–75, Canadian authorities, following the Federal Reserve's example, began to emphasize the money growth rate as the proximate target of monetary policy. But, this shift in the intellectual basis and operational target of monetary policy was not a fundamental change. The substantive aim of policy remained the same as before—to stabilize Canadian costs and prices relative to U.S. costs and prices.[21] And, keeping Canadian prices in line with U.S. prices through monetary policy necessarily implies a stable exchange rate with the U.S. dollar.

Canada, in sum, was a textbook example of a country on the pure U.S. dollar standard during the period of the Great Inflation. Accordingly, Canada's price experience in 1968–75 mirrored that of the United States (see Table 5-1, p. 26). A tighter monetary policy in Canada would have allowed the Canadian dollar to float up, shielding the economy from inflation in the United States. But, if the Bank of Canada had followed a less expansive policy than the Federal Reserve, Canadian export- and import-competing industries might have been damaged as the Canadian dollar rose temporarily above a level consistent with comparative U.S. and Canadian prices. When the chips were down, the Canadian authorities deliberately chose imported inflation as the lesser evil.[22]

## JAPAN

Like Canada, Japan largely accepted imported inflation in the period 1968–75, neither greatly amplifying it as Britain did, nor resisting it as Germany did.

Beginning in 1967, as U.S. prices accelerated and prices in Japan followed suit, Japan's overall balance of payments developed a persistent surplus that seems to have been caused in part by a rising demand for (nominal) money balances associated with imported inflation (see Chart 6-5).[23] Late in 1969, the Japanese authorities saw themselves confronted with a dilemma. Accelerating prices seemed to call for tighter money but tighter money would aggravate the balance-of-payments surplus, which the Japanese were beginning to consider a threat to the yen exchange rate and a political liability in relations with the United States. They accordingly resorted to fiscal measures in an attempt to slow the economy

---

20 See, e.g., Annual Report of the Governor of the Bank of Canada to the Minister of Finance (1968), p. 35.

21 See, e.g., Annual Report of the Governor of the Bank of Canada to the Minister of Finance (1975), p. 12.

22 See Annual Report of the Governor of the Bank of Canada to the Minister of Finance (1971), pp. 6–7.

23 Another factor that may help to account for the emergence of a payments surplus in 1967 was a sustained acceleration of real output, which doubtless contributed to the rise in Japanese money demand. In the three years 1967–69, Japan's real GNP grew at an average annual rate of 12.5 percent—up from about 9.5 percent in the preceding four-year period.

**CHART 6-5**

**Sources of the Japanese Monetary Base**

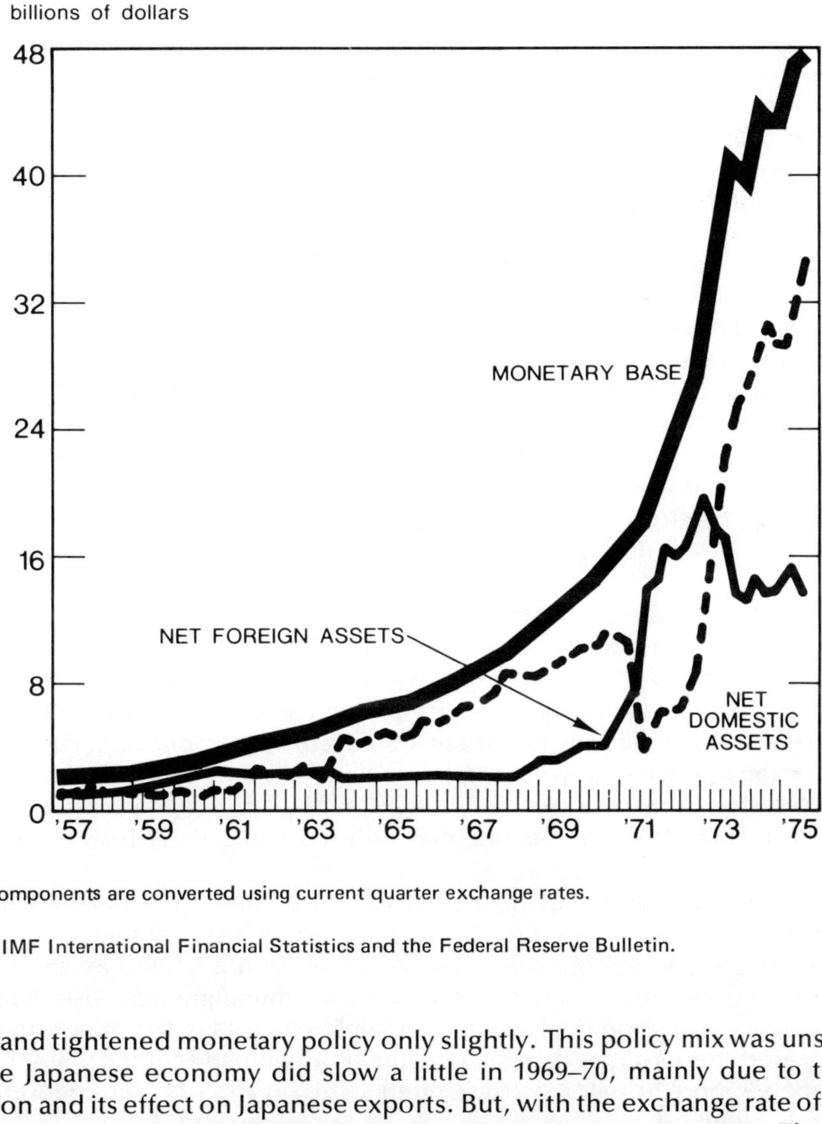


Note: Components are converted using current quarter exchange rates.

Source: IMF International Financial Statistics and the Federal Reserve Bulletin.

down, and tightened monetary policy only slightly. This policy mix was unsuccessful. The Japanese economy did slow a little in 1969–70, mainly due to the U.S. recession and its effect on Japanese exports. But, with the exchange rate of the yen fixed, inflation continued to accelerate in line with prices overseas. The overall surplus in the balance of payments increased in 1969–70 as the domestic demand for (nominal) money rose with the price level, while the pace of domestic credit expansion slowed a little.

Japan's monetary policy was relaxed again in third quarter 1970. But, the payments surplus continued to grow because U.S. monetary policy had now been greatly eased. The growth of the Japanese money supply accelerated and by the spring of 1971, there were signs that the economy was beginning to respond normally to monetary stimulus. Then came the dramatic events of August 15, 1971, when the United States suspended the gold convertibility of the dollar, imposed an import surcharge and demanded a large revaluation of the yen. The psychological impact of these developments on the Japanese business community was extraordinary. The "Nixon shock," as it was called in Japan, was something close to a collective nervous breakdown. Output slowed sharply as investment plans were scaled down or cancelled by firms whose managers feared that the U.S. moves presaged an all-out assault on Japanese exports. The demand for precautionary money balances rose steeply.[24]

The authorities' response was to move quickly and decisively to a highly expansive monetary and fiscal policy. They were motivated not only by the desire to meet the sudden rise in private demand for liquidity and to counter the recession, but also by a need to eliminate the balance-of-payments surplus, which they now saw as a serious provocation to the United States. The only way to ease U.S. pressure for restrictions on Japanese exports and a higher yen, it seemed, was to eliminate the payments surplus. Accordingly, domestic interest rates were forced down sharply. A series of regular and supplementary budgets was adopted in 1971 and 1972, causing deficits to rise to heights previously unimagined in Japan.[25] Given the authorities' desire to push interest rates down and the unusually strong private demand for liquidity, deficit financing on a large scale inevitably led to an explosive rise in domestic credit (see Chart 6-5). The narrowly defined money supply speeded up from an 18 percent growth rate in 1970 to an annual average of 24 percent in 1971 and 1972.

The rapid expansion of domestic credit in 1971–72 in the wake of the "Nixon shock" may have created monetary conditions in Japan that were, for a time at least, more expansive than in the United States. Evidence tending to support this conclusion is that inflation in Japan rose well above U.S. inflation in 1973 and 1974, even if allowance is made for the normal (nonmonetary) differential between Japanese and U.S. inflation, as measured by consumer prices.[26] Furthermore, Japan's overall balance of payments fell into deficit in 1973 and 1974, while the yen depreciated sharply against the dollar in 1974. This also suggests that monetary conditions in Japan may have been temporarily more expansive than in the United States.

The more rapid rise in Japanese prices in 1973–74 may also have been due in large part to nonmonetary causes. Thus, the oil price increase had a much larger immediate impact on energy prices in Japan than in the United States, because Japan's dependence for energy on imported oil is much greater. Also, consumer prices in Japan are a good deal more sensitive to changes in the prices of internationally traded commodities than are consumer prices in the United States because Japan depends more heavily than the United States on imports of commodities. So, when world commodity prices rise, as they did strongly in 1973 and 1974, Japanese

---

24 Japanese "[b]usinesses appeared to increase their liquidity preferences, in view of mounting uncertainties, particularly the international monetary unrest." Report of the Economic Planning Agency for Fiscal Year 1971, p. 51.

25 The ratio of the deficit to expenditures in fiscal year 1972 was "the highest of the postwar period." Report of the Economic Planning Agency for Fiscal Year 1972, p. 37.

26 See Table 5-1, p. 26.

## CHART 6-6

### Differences in Monetary Conditions in Japan and the United States: 1955–75

**Japanese and U.S. money growth rates:**
**Actual and adjusted for trend growth rates of real GNP**

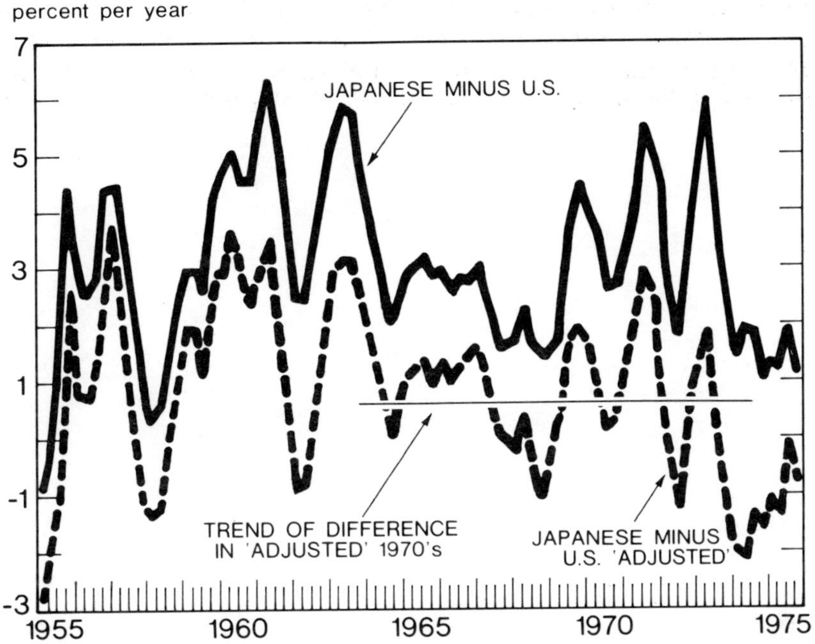


Note: Each country's money series was adjusted for differences in money demand by subtracting a 12-quarter moving average of real GNP growth from the 3-quarter moving average of money supply growth.

Source: Appendix Tables.

consumer prices rise for a time relative to U.S. prices, without regard to relative monetary conditions in the two countries.

Further evidence of U.S. and Japanese monetary conditions is given in Chart 6-6. It compares U.S. and Japanese money growth rates, after adjustment for differences in the demand for money. A 12-quarter moving average of real GNP growth is used as a proxy for the growth of money demand. This comparison suggests that monetary conditions in Japan may have been a bit more expansive than in the United States in 1969–71 but that for the whole period 1968–75, conditions in the two countries were, on average, about the same.[27] The latter conclusion is consistent with the evolution of the yen-dollar exchange rate. Between 1971

27 See the similar chart comparing monetary conditions in Germany and the United States, Chart 6-3, p. 37.

and 1975, the yen first rose sharply against the dollar and then fell (in 1974) to stabilize at about Y 300 to the dollar—a net rise of some 20 percent as compared with its starting point of Y 360. If monetary conditions in Japan in that period had been on average more expansive than in the United States, so large an appreciation would hardly have occurred even if one assumes that the yen was initially undervalued against the dollar.

In sum, Japan belongs to that group of countries whose role in the Great Inflation was more passive than active. The Japanese authorities' devotion to a fixed exchange rate, their desire to resist U.S. pressure for a revalued yen and their exaggerated fear of the effect of a higher exchange rate on exports led them to import the U.S. inflation and perhaps to amplify it a little.

# Conclusion 7

If inflation is essentially a matter of too much money, the Great Inflation is no great mystery. The acceleration of prices that was the common experience of all the industrial countries in the late sixties and early seventies was caused by an antecedent rise of the money stock in these countries. In 1973–74, exogenous supply shocks—particularly the OPEC decisions that quintupled the price of oil and the crop failures in the United States and the Soviet Union—helped speed the rise in prices everywhere. But, they probably did not increase substantially, if at all, the cumulative rise in the price level of the industrial countries over the whole period 1968–75.

This much of the story of the Great Inflation as we have told it would probably be accepted by most economists—or at least by those of a monetary persuasion. But, the question of where the inflationary money growth came from is more controversial.

The argument of this essay is that an overly expansive U.S. monetary policy, working through fixed exchange rates and the dollar standard, was responsible for the major part of money growth—and hence of price inflation—in the industrial world. This is a statement about causation. It does not imply that the United States was more responsible than other countries in a political or moral sense. Other countries could have shielded themselves from imported inflation by allowing their currencies to appreciate against the dollar and by following domestic monetary policies more moderate than those of the United States. But, among the larger countries, only Germany took this course. The others passively suffered imported inflation, or amplified it by domestic credit expansion more rapid than in the United States.

How U.S. monetary policy and the workings of the Bretton Woods system caused much of the world's inflation is easier to understand when it is seen in historical perspective. The Great Inflation is unique, historically, because it was the first major, peacetime inflation in modern times that was international in scope. Before the Bretton Woods system, international monetary systems were generally subject to the rule of gold convertibility; that is, the currencies of the leading countries were normally convertible into gold at fixed rates. Thus, the world's monetary base was tied to the world's supply of monetary gold. In such monetary systems, rapid, prolonged inflation on an international scale was impossible, except during or immediately after major wars in which gold convertibility had been suspended and the money stocks of the belligerents had grown rapidly, under the exigencies of wartime finance.

Unlike the pre-World War II systems, the Bretton Woods system included a monetary mechanism that was capable of expanding the monetary base in the industrial world at a rapid pace, even in peacetime. That mechanism was the dollar standard. Reserve currencies had existed before World War II, but they had normally been subject to the rule of convertibility. Even in the Bretton Woods system, the dollar was nominally convertible into gold for official settlements. But, from the early 1960s on, gold convertibility became increasingly fictitious, and it was virtually suspended in March 1968. As a result, the U.S. Federal Reserve was able to act as a world central bank; its monetary liabilities provided the basis for monetary expansion in other countries. Other countries accepted this mechanism without fully appreciating its potential for monetary expansion. They did so, no doubt, because the mechanism was inseparable from the central feature of the Bretton Woods system: the pegging of other currencies at fixed rates to the U.S. dollar.

## U.S. MONETARY POLICY, THROWN OFF COURSE, LEADS TO WORLD INFLATION

Nevertheless, all went well until the mid-1960s, because U.S. monetary policy was on a moderate course. In this period, the dollar standard was a source of monetary and price stability for the industrial world as a whole. Beginning in 1965, however, U.S. monetary policy was thrown off course by the decisions of the Johnson Administration to finance the Vietnam War and the Administration's domestic programs, mainly by monetary expansion. From 1965 on, U.S. monetary management went from bad to worse. In 1969, the Federal Reserve tried to kill inflation quickly, and this brought on the 1970 recession. The 1970 recession was accompanied by inflation, shored up by the momentum of inflationary expectations left over from the run up of inflation after 1965. With inflationary expectations high, the monetary expansion needed to speed recovery in 1971–72 was unprecedented. The fateful decision of the Federal Reserve and the Administration to take this course—a decision apparently made with little foresight of the international consequences—gave to world inflation the dimensions that justify the adjective "Great."

In the first phase of the Great Inflation, inflation in the other industrial countries was mainly imported from the United States, although expansive domestic credit policies in Britain and France, along with large devaluations of the pound and the franc, led to higher inflation in those countries than in the United States. Beginning in 1971, the policy responses of the main industrial countries began to diverge. Canada and Japan continued to follow policies that caused domestic monetary conditions to follow more or less closely conditions in the United States. But, Germany followed a restrictive domestic credit policy and allowed the mark to appreciate against the dollar, thereby holding inflation below that of the United States. Britain took the opposite tack. Like their U.S. counterparts only more so, the British authorities responded to "stagflation" in 1970–71 with an extreme dose of fiscal deficits and monetary expansion. They were soon forced by the balance-of-payments effects of these measures to allow the pound to float. Thereafter, Britain's highly expansive monetary policy was largely reflected in British prices, which soared well above those of other industrial countries in 1974–75.

The reluctance of most countries to allow their exchange rates to rise against the dollar in part reflected a traditional attachment to fixed exchange rates. But, it was also political; the authorities in Europe, Canada and Japan were naturally sensitive to export interests. They also believed that, in a period of business slowdown such as 1970–71, a rise in the exchange rate would increase unemployment. These fears were not without a basis in economic theory, but they were probably exaggerated. In retrospect, it appears that far too high a price was paid in inflation to avoid exchange-rate changes whose impact on exports and employment would probably have been marginal.

Money growth in the 10 leading industrial countries slowed from an average of 12 percent per annum in 1971–72 to 7½ percent in 1974, as the United States and other industrial countries launched simultaneously a monetary offensive against inflation. The turn to monetary restraint was probably too abrupt. Policymakers, in most of the industrial countries, impressed by the unexpected severity of inflation, did not take seriously enough contemporary warnings that the oil price hike would have a substantial, if temporary, depressing effect on real money balances, real income, business activity, and employment. Be that as it may, it was the collision between the rapid deceleration of money growth in the industrial countries and the steep run up in prices in 1973–75—due in part to the oil price hike—that produced the worst of the postwar recessions and brought the drama of the Great Inflation to a close.

# Epilogue 8

Since late 1974 or early 1975, with inflation slowing, monetary policies in the industrial countries have eased again. But, this time the United States, profiting by the experience of 1971–72, has been the most cautious of all the industrial countries (except Switzerland). Japanese monetary policy has also been moderate, apparently aimed at stabilizing the yen-dollar exchange rate in the neighborhood of Y 300. Canada's monetary policy since 1974 has been more erratic than U.S. or Japanese policy, but still seems to be aimed at keeping the Canadian dollar close to par with the U.S. dollar, in the longer run. Monetary conditions in these three countries are accordingly likely to converge on a norm of relative stability established by the United States. In Europe, conditions are more varied and will probably remain so, as the European countries have not, in general, attempted to stabilize their exchange rates against the dollar. In consequence, European monetary conditions in the last three years have been heavily influenced by domestic fiscal and monetary policies which have varied considerably from country to country.

In the last two years, then, there has been a shift of monetary roles between the United States and the other industrial countries. By virtue of the relative moderation of its monetary policy, the United States has changed from a source of inflation to a force—actual or potential—for relative price stability. In the case of Canada and Japan, because these countries have chosen to stabilize their currencies against the dollar, the stabilizing influence of U.S. monetary conditions is actual. For much of Europe, it remains potential only because domestic political priorities favor an inflationary course, as in Britain, Italy and France. Germany, too, is a source of relative price stability for the countries which stabilize their currencies against the mark in the European currency "snake."

If the United States cleaves to its present line of monetary moderation and weathers the coming recovery without an acceleration of money growth and inflation, the present situation holds out the promise of longer-run improvement of price stability on an international scale. Britain, Italy and France will doubtless remain for the foreseeable future outside this trend. But, in time, the mark would probably be stabilized against the dollar and with it the other currencies of the European "snake." The result would be a monetary system capable of giving a large part of the industrial world (the United States, Canada, Japan, and the countries participating in the European "snake," as well as Switzerland) a measure of stability in prices and exchange rates considerably greater than in the early 1970s.

To revert to the main theme of this report: the general rate of world inflation depends heavily on monetary conditions in the reserve center. Some other countries may be prevented, by political necessity, from having as much monetary stability as policies of the reserve center make possible. A few, like Switzerland, may be able, by allowing their exchange rates to float and following a more cautious monetary policy, to have more price stability than the United States. But, as long as the world remains on a dollar standard, only the United States has it within its power to safeguard—or undermine—the general stability of the system as a whole.

# Appendix Tables

## TABLE A-1

**Inflation (Consumer Price Index): Annual or Annualized Percentage Changes of Period Averages for Select Countries**

| From Prior Year in Percent | | U.S. | Canada | Japan | U.K. | Germany | France | Italy | Netherlds | Belgium | Switzld | 10 Countries Combined |
|---|---|---|---|---|---|---|---|---|---|---|---|---|
| Weights | | .4705 | .0518 | .1257 | .0630 | .1108 | .0830 | .0481 | .0192 | .0150 | .0130 | |
| Actual | 1960 | 1.5 | 1.3 | 3.7 | 1.0 | 1.5 | 4.1 | 2.3 | 2.7 | 0.3 | 1.4 | 2.0 |
| | 1961 | 1.1 | 0.9 | 5.2 | 3.5 | 2.3 | 2.4 | 2.1 | 1.2 | 1.0 | 1.9 | 2.0 |
| | 1962 | 1.2 | 1.2 | 6.8 | 4.1 | 3.0 | 5.2 | 4.7 | 2.4 | 1.4 | 4.3 | 2.8 |
| | 1963 | 1.2 | 1.7 | 6.3 | 2.1 | 3.0 | 5.0 | 7.4 | 3.2 | 2.1 | 3.4 | 2.8 |
| | 1964 | 1.3 | 1.8 | 3.8 | 3.2 | 2.3 | 3.2 | 5.9 | 5.9 | 4.2 | 3.1 | 2.4 |
| | 1965 | 1.6 | 2.4 | 6.7 | 4.8 | 3.3 | 2.7 | 4.5 | 4.8 | 4.1 | 3.4 | 3.0 |
| | 1966 | 3.0 | 3.8 | 5.0 | 3.8 | 3.5 | 2.6 | 2.4 | 5.7 | 4.2 | 4.7 | 3.4 |
| | 1967 | 2.8 | 3.6 | 4.0 | 2.6 | 1.7 | 2.8 | 3.2 | 3.5 | 2.9 | 4.0 | 2.9 |
| | 1968 | 4.2 | 4.1 | 5.3 | 4.7 | 1.7 | 4.5 | 1.3 | 3.7 | 2.7 | 2.4 | 3.9 |
| | 1969 | 5.4 | 4.5 | 5.3 | 5.4 | 3.1 | 6.0 | 2.7 | 7.4 | 3.7 | 2.5 | 5.0 |
| | 1970 | 5.9 | 3.4 | 7.6 | 6.4 | 3.3 | 5.8 | 4.9 | 3.6 | 4.0 | 3.6 | 5.6 |
| | 1971 | 4.3 | 2.8 | 6.1 | 9.4 | 5.3 | 5.4 | 5.0 | 7.5 | 4.3 | 6.6 | 5.1 |
| | 1972 | 3.3 | 4.8 | 4.5 | 7.1 | 5.5 | 9.2 | 5.6 | 7.8 | 5.5 | 6.7 | 4.8 |
| | 1973 | 6.2 | 7.6 | 11.8 | 9.2 | 6.9 | 7.4 | 10.8 | 8.0 | 6.9 | 8.7 | 7.7 |
| | 1974 | 11.0 | 10.9 | 24.4 | 16.0 | 7.0 | 13.5 | 19.2 | 9.6 | 12.7 | 9.8 | 13.2 |
| | 1975 | 9.2 | 10.7 | 11.9 | 24.3 | 5.9 | 11.8 | 17.0 | 10.2 | 12.8 | 6.7 | 10.8 |

(Continued)

## TABLE A-1 (Continued)

| From Prior Quarter in Percent (SAAR) | | U.S. | Canada | Japan | U.K. | Germany | France | Italy | Netherlds | Belgium | Switzld | 10 Countries Combined |
|---|---|---|---|---|---|---|---|---|---|---|---|---|
| Quarter | 1971 1 | 3.5 | 2.2 | 6.0 | 10.5 | 7.3 | 4.1 | 4.2 | 9.8 | 4.1 | 6.4 | 4.9 |
| | 2 | 4.1 | 5.6 | 5.1 | 11.7 | 5.9 | 7.1 | 4.8 | 10.5 | 5.7 | 7.4 | 5.4 |
| | 3 | 3.9 | 6.1 | 6.6 | 8.8 | 5.9 | 6.2 | 5.4 | 4.8 | 5.7 | 6.5 | 5.2 |
| | 4 | 2.4 | 2.8 | 3.8 | 5.4 | 4.2 | 6.0 | 5.1 | 7.7 | 5.5 | 5.4 | 3.6 |
| | 1972 1 | 3.7 | 4.8 | 2.6 | 6.5 | 5.3 | 16.9 | 4.0 | 8.8 | 4.4 | 7.0 | 5.2 |
| | 2 | 2.7 | 3.5 | 4.9 | 3.7 | 4.5 | 6.3 | 4.9 | 10.2 | 4.4 | 7.3 | 3.9 |
| | 3 | 3.5 | 8.2 | 6.3 | 10.7 | 8.3 | 8.2 | 8.3 | 2.9 | 7.7 | 7.1 | 5.8 |
| | 4 | 3.9 | 4.1 | 4.7 | 10.6 | 7.0 | 8.8 | 11.3 | 10.6 | 8.1 | 6.4 | 5.8 |
| | 1973 1 | 6.2 | 7.6 | 13.4 | 6.8 | 5.7 | 2.8 | 10.5 | 7.1 | 7.3 | 9.8 | 7.1 |
| | 2 | 8.6 | 9.4 | 17.1 | 9.0 | 8.2 | 8.4 | 14.5 | 12.3 | 5.7 | 9.3 | 10.0 |
| | 3 | 8.9 | 11.7 | 16.4 | 10.7 | 6.6 | 10.9 | 10.4 | 3.2 | 5.8 | 8.1 | 9.9 |
| | 4 | 9.8 | 7.4 | 19.4 | 14.9 | 8.3 | 11.3 | 11.5 | 9.6 | 8.7 | 16.0 | 11.3 |
| | 1974 1 | 12.3 | 10.1 | 47.7 | 16.7 | 6.7 | 14.9 | 21.9 | 9.9 | 14.2 | 8.4 | 16.9 |
| | 2 | 11.3 | 13.7 | 14.5 | 21.2 | 6.9 | 17.1 | 22.4 | 12.7 | 17.8 | 5.6 | 13.0 |
| | 3 | 12.5 | 12.7 | 20.0 | 15.5 | 6.2 | 13.1 | 27.2 | 7.3 | 18.1 | 12.8 | 13.7 |
| | 4 | 12.4 | 11.3 | 18.7 | 19.3 | 6.4 | 14.8 | 27.6 | 13.7 | 13.7 | 8.2 | 13.8 |
| | 1975 1 | 8.1 | 8.9 | 3.0 | 26.0 | 4.5 | 10.7 | 14.6 | 8.8 | 11.7 | 5.4 | 8.8 |
| | 2 | 6.2 | 9.0 | 14.0 | 37.6 | 7.8 | 10.4 | 10.1 | 11.6 | 10.7 | 7.8 | 10.2 |
| | 3 | 8.3 | 14.3 | 9.0 | 23.9 | 5.6 | 9.6 | 9.6 | 8.1 | 9.7 | 4.1 | 9.5 |
| | 4 | 6.6 | 8.2 | 11.2 | 14.9 | 4.0 | 8.3 | 11.2 | 9.4 | 12.7 | –1.2 | 7.9 |

Date: 9 July 1976.

## TABLE A-2

**Money Supply for Narrowly Defined Period Averages:**
**Annual or Annualized Percentage Changes of Period Averages for Select Countries**

| From Prior Year in Percent | | U.S. | Canada | Japan | U.K. | Germany | France | Italy | Netherlds | Belgium | Switzld | 10 Countries Combined |
|---|---|---|---|---|---|---|---|---|---|---|---|---|
| Weights | | .4705 | .0518 | .1257 | .0630 | .1108 | .0830 | .0481 | .0192 | .0150 | .0130 | |
| Actual | 1960 | −0.1 | 1.3 | 19.9 | 3.3 | 9.3 | 11.2 | 13.0 | 5.2 | 2.1 | 7.3 | 5.5 |
| | 1961 | 2.1 | 5.2 | 25.1 | 0.7 | 9.3 | 16.4 | 14.1 | 7.8 | 5.2 | 14.7 | 8.0 |
| | 1962 | 2.2 | 3.3 | 16.0 | −0.0 | 11.0 | 16.9 | 17.8 | 5.7 | 7.0 | 10.4 | 7.0 |
| | 1963 | 2.9 | 5.9 | 26.4 | 6.2 | 7.3 | 16.7 | 17.1 | 9.7 | 9.9 | 8.0 | 8.8 |
| | 1964 | 4.0 | 5.1 | 16.8 | 5.4 | 8.4 | 10.1 | 7.3 | 8.5 | 5.6 | 5.5 | 7.0 |
| | 1965 | 4.3 | 6.3 | 16.8 | 3.1 | 8.9 | 9.1 | 12.7 | 10.9 | 7.8 | 4.5 | 7.4 |
| | 1966 | 4.6 | 6.9 | 16.3 | 3.1 | 4.3 | 8.9 | 15.1 | 7.2 | 6.7 | 2.6 | 7.0 |
| | 1967 | 4.0 | 9.7 | 13.4 | 3.8 | 3.4 | 7.1 | 13.1 | 7.0 | 4.3 | 3.0 | 6.1 |
| | 1968 | 7.1 | 4.3 | 14.6 | 4.6 | 7.5 | 5.7 | 13.3 | 8.8 | 6.6 | 9.5 | 8.0 |
| | 1969 | 6.0 | 7.5 | 18.4 | 5.2 | 8.2 | 4.3 | 15.1 | 9.5 | 4.8 | 5.4 | 8.2 |
| | 1970 | 3.9 | 2.2 | 18.3 | 6.7 | 6.5 | 0.2 | 21.7 | 10.6 | 5.6 | 4.9 | 6.8 |
| | 1971 | 6.7 | 12.8 | 25.5 | 12.9 | 11.7 | 13.5 | 22.8 | 16.7 | 9.9 | 16.5 | 12.0 |
| | 1972 | 7.1 | 13.9 | 22.0 | 14.7 | 13.8 | 12.9 | 17.9 | 17.8 | 12.7 | 17.5 | 12.0 |
| | 1973 | 7.5 | 14.5 | 26.2 | 8.6 | 5.9 | 10.8 | 21.1 | 7.4 | 12.7 | 2.2 | 11.0 |
| | 1974 | 5.5 | 9.8 | 13.2 | 5.5 | 6.0 | 10.8 | 17.1 | 3.1 | 8.6 | 0.1 | 7.6 |
| | 1975 | 4.2 | 13.7 | 10.4 | 16.3 | 14.1 | 11.8 | 7.7 | 18.6 | 11.7 | 4.6 | 8.5 |

(Continued)

TABLE A-2 (Continued)

| From Prior Quarter in Percent (SAAR) | | | U.S. | Canada | Japan | U.K. | Germany | France | Italy | Netherlds | Belgium | Switzld | 10 Countries Combined |
|---|---|---|---|---|---|---|---|---|---|---|---|---|---|
| Quarter | 1971 | 1 | 7.0 | 17.9 | 31.1 | 17.6 | 12.9 | 13.8 | 25.0 | 21.4 | 9.4 | 16.7 | 13.8 |
| | | 2 | 10.5 | 19.4 | 29.7 | 2.9 | 13.4 | 10.2 | 16.4 | 15.3 | 9.0 | 24.0 | 13.7 |
| | | 3 | 6.8 | 15.3 | 39.1 | 14.5 | 17.9 | 15.2 | 21.7 | 12.8 | 16.2 | 28.6 | 15.0 |
| | | 4 | 2.6 | 17.4 | 20.4 | 21.5 | 8.7 | 10.5 | 17.6 | 14.6 | 9.5 | 22.7 | 9.4 |
| | 1972 | 1 | 7.4 | 10.6 | 17.4 | 15.8 | 12.9 | 7.6 | 18.3 | 18.0 | 10.9 | 27.9 | 11.0 |
| | | 2 | 8.4 | 9.0 | 13.6 | 15.1 | 15.4 | 15.0 | 18.3 | 22.3 | 15.7 | 4.2 | 11.6 |
| | | 3 | 8.7 | 17.5 | 17.3 | 7.1 | 19.3 | 22.7 | 14.1 | 29.5 | 13.7 | 10.7 | 13.2 |
| | | 4 | 9.3 | 17.6 | 46.1 | 18.1 | 9.6 | 15.0 | 18.7 | 3.2 | 14.9 | -2.3 | 15.7 |
| | 1973 | 1 | 7.5 | 15.7 | 30.0 | 0.3 | 8.9 | 2.6 | 21.1 | 15.4 | 13.3 | 1.7 | 10.9 |
| | | 2 | 6.5 | 14.1 | 29.8 | 23.6 | -2.4 | 16.2 | 26.0 | 3.0 | 13.9 | 2.9 | 11.7 |
| | | 3 | 5.7 | 13.7 | 13.1 | -12.6 | -8.7 | 0.5 | 25.4 | -15.7 | 5.9 | -0.1 | 4.3 |
| | | 4 | 5.2 | 4.0 | 7.9 | 18.7 | 6.7 | 12.5 | 20.3 | 2.4 | 10.6 | 2.8 | 7.8 |
| | 1974 | 1 | 6.1 | 14.5 | 16.1 | -11.7 | 8.6 | 11.5 | 17.3 | 4.8 | 8.3 | -3.9 | 7.8 |
| | | 2 | 5.7 | 20.0 | 17.6 | 8.8 | 8.7 | 16.8 | 16.0 | 6.6 | 10.0 | 1.1 | 9.9 |
| | | 3 | 4.3 | -5.5 | 6.2 | 18.8 | 12.2 | -2.4 | 9.7 | 9.3 | 2.8 | -0.5 | 5.5 |
| | | 4 | 4.1 | 1.6 | 4.9 | 33.0 | 13.0 | 30.6 | 4.4 | 18.6 | 12.8 | 4.5 | 9.5 |
| | 1975 | 1 | 0.6 | 26.5 | 15.4 | 8.8 | 11.4 | 4.0 | 10.9 | 13.1 | 10.6 | 8.4 | 6.7 |
| | | 2 | 7.6 | 12.3 | 7.0 | 8.0 | 17.6 | 3.4 | -11.4 | 32.4 | 16.3 | 6.8 | 8.2 |
| | | 3 | 7.2 | 20.2 | 16.7 | 26.2 | 16.9 | 22.3 | 28.7 | 31.7 | 15.5 | -0.9 | 14.1 |
| | | 4 | 2.3 | 30.3 | 7.6 | 11.7 | 20.0 | 23.5 | 18.5 | 7.2 | 13.3 | 9.6 | 9.9 |

Date: 9 July 1976.

## TABLE A-3

**Real GNP: Annual or Annualized Percentage Changes of Period Averages for Select Countries**

| From Prior Year in Percent | | U.S. | Canada | Japan | U.K. | Germany | France | Italy | Netherlds | Belgium | Switzld | 10 Countries Combined |
|---|---|---|---|---|---|---|---|---|---|---|---|---|
| Weights | | .4705 | .0518 | .1257 | .0630 | .1108 | .0830 | .0481 | .0192 | .0150 | .0130 | |
| Actual | 1960 | 2.3 | 2.9 | 13.2 | 5.0 | 16.3 | 8.6 | 6.1 | 8.3 | 6.2 | 8.2 | 6.4 |
| | 1961 | 2.5 | 2.8 | 14.4 | 3.8 | 7.5 | 5.9 | 9.0 | 3.6 | 4.9 | 9.8 | 5.4 |
| | 1962 | 5.8 | 6.8 | 7.0 | 1.0 | 7.1 | 7.5 | 7.4 | 4.5 | 5.5 | 6.3 | 6.0 |
| | 1963 | 4.0 | 5.2 | 10.3 | 4.7 | 3.6 | 6.1 | 6.6 | 5.5 | 5.2 | 5.9 | 5.2 |
| | 1964 | 5.3 | 6.7 | 13.2 | 6.0 | 7.1 | 7.9 | 3.3 | 11.1 | 7.3 | 6.8 | 6.9 |
| | 1965 | 5.9 | 6.7 | 5.2 | 2.4 | 6.1 | 4.8 | 3.0 | 6.4 | 4.9 | 4.4 | 5.4 |
| | 1966 | 6.0 | 6.9 | 9.8 | 2.0 | 2.9 | 5.9 | 5.7 | 2.7 | 3.2 | 2.3 | 5.7 |
| | 1967 | 2.7 | 3.3 | 12.9 | 2.3 | -0.2 | 5.4 | 6.5 | 6.3 | 4.1 | 2.9 | 4.2 |
| | 1968 | 4.4 | 5.8 | 13.4 | 3.7 | 7.3 | 4.8 | 6.6 | 6.5 | 4.2 | 4.8 | 6.1 |
| | 1969 | 2.6 | 5.2 | 10.8 | 1.8 | 8.2 | 8.0 | 7.3 | 5.4 | 6.9 | 5.5 | 5.2 |
| | 1970 | -0.3 | 2.6 | 11.1 | 1.9 | 5.8 | 6.0 | 4.9 | 7.5 | 7.5 | 6.3 | 3.3 |
| | 1971 | 3.0 | 5.7 | 7.4 | 2.3 | 3.0 | 5.6 | 1.6 | 4.7 | 4.8 | 7.5 | 4.0 |
| | 1972 | 5.7 | 6.0 | 8.9 | 1.7 | 3.4 | 6.1 | 3.1 | 5.6 | 5.8 | 8.0 | 5.6 |
| | 1973 | 5.3 | 6.9 | 9.8 | 5.4 | 5.1 | 6.3 | 5.9 | 5.2 | 5.8 | 3.8 | 6.0 |
| | 1974 | -1.8 | 2.8 | -1.1 | 0.5 | 0.4 | 3.2 | 4.2 | 3.8 | 4.2 | 2.1 | -0.1 |
| | 1975 | -2.0 | 0.2 | 2.2 | -1.6 | -3.4 | -3.5 | -3.8 | -1.8 | -2.5 | -7.0 | -1.8 |

(Continued)

## TABLE A-3 (Continued)

| From Prior Quarter in Percent (SAAR) | | U.S. | Canada | Japan | U.K. | Germany | France | Italy | Netherlds | Belgium | Switzld | 10 Countries Combined |
|---|---|---|---|---|---|---|---|---|---|---|---|---|
| Quarter | 1971 1 | 9.2 | 9.2 | 10.2 | –4.7 | 0.6 | 1.0 | 1.0 | | | | |
| | 2 | 3.0 | 8.4 | 5.9 | 7.0 | 0.9 | 7.1 | –2.5 | | | | |
| | 3 | 2.8 | 10.3 | 8.9 | 8.6 | 3.9 | 6.5 | –1.5 | | | | |
| | 4 | 3.5 | 4.2 | 4.6 | 0.1 | –2.9 | 8.1 | 12.8 | | | | |
| | 1972 1 | 7.6 | 2.8 | 14.3 | –7.3 | 9.4 | 8.5 | 4.7 | | | | |
| | 2 | 7.9 | 11.5 | 2.3 | 11.3 | 0.3 | –0.7 | –1.9 | | | | |
| | 3 | 5.3 | 1.1 | 14.6 | –2.0 | 2.9 | 7.1 | –3.4 | | | | |
| | 4 | 8.5 | 8.3 | 13.9 | 8.5 | 8.5 | 9.0 | 13.5 | | | | |
| | 1973 1 | 8.8 | 11.2 | 15.9 | 23.2 | 12.2 | 9.4 | –4.1 | | | | |
| | 2 | 0.2 | 3.4 | 7.3 | –8.0 | –0.5 | 3.8 | 20.0 | | (Quarterly data | | |
| | 3 | 2.7 | 5.2 | 0.3 | –0.0 | 1.9 | 2.6 | 9.7 | | not available) | | |
| | 4 | 1.4 | 7.3 | 0.2 | –3.7 | 1.4 | 6.2 | 5.1 | | | | |
| | 1974 1 | –3.9 | 3.6 | –11.5 | –5.4 | 3.5 | 6.6 | 4.0 | | | | |
| | 2 | –3.7 | –1.3 | 4.5 | 15.1 | –1.6 | 1.5 | 15.8 | | | | |
| | 3 | –2.3 | 0.1 | 4.6 | 7.0 | –1.3 | 2.4 | –16.9 | | | | |
| | 4 | –7.5 | –1.1 | 0.9 | –5.9 | –7.1 | –10.2 | –8.2 | | | | |
| | 1975 1 | –9.2 | –3.1 | –1.0 | –2.6 | –10.1 | –11.5 | –1.7 | | | | |
| | 2 | 3.3 | 3.4 | 4.3 | –9.4 | 0.4 | 4.3 | –4.4 | | | | |
| | 3 | 11.9 | 4.2 | 3.5 | –1.9 | 0.0 | –0.7 | –0.2 | | | | |
| | 4 | 5.0 | 1.4 | 2.9 | 9.5 | 13.2 | 7.0 | 7.7 | | | | |

Date: 9 July 1976.

# National Planning Association

NPA is an independent, private, nonprofit, nonpolitical organization that carries on research and policy formulation in the public interest. NPA was founded during the Great Depression of the 1930s when conflicts among the major economic groups—business, farmers, labor—threatened to paralyze national decision making on the critical issues confronting American society. It was dedicated, in the words of its statement of purpose, to the task "of getting (these) diverse groups to work together . . . to narrow areas of controversy and broaden areas of agreement . . . (and) to provide on specific problems concrete programs for action planned in the best traditions of a functioning democracy." From the beginning, NPA has been committed to the view that the survival of a functioning American democracy under the increasingly rigorous conditions of the 20th century could not be assured only by more effective governmental policies and programs. Equally essential, NPA believes, are the preservation of private economic initiative and activity dispersed throughout the society and the continuous development by the major private groups of a substantial consensus on how to cope with the problems confronting the nation at home and abroad.

NPA brings together influential and knowledgeable leaders from business, labor, agriculture, and the applied and academic professions to serve on policy committees. These committees analyze and agree upon recommendations for dealing with domestic and international developments affecting the well-being of the United States. The research and writing for these committees are provided by NPA's professional staff and, as required, by outside experts.

In addition, NPA's professional staff undertakes a wide variety of technical research activities designed to provide data and ideas for policy makers and planners in government and the private sector. These activities include the preparation on a regular basis of economic and demographic projections for the national economy, regions, states, and metropolitan areas; program planning and evaluation for federal, state and local agencies; research on national goals and priorities; planning studies for manpower training, vocational education, medical care, environmental protection, energy needs, and other economic and social problems confronting American society; and analyses and forecasts of changing international realities and their implications for U.S. policies. In developing its staff capabilities, NPA has increasingly emphasized two related qualifications—the interdisciplinary knowledge required to understand the complex nature of many real-life problems, and the ability to bridge the gap between the theoretical or highly technical research of the universities and other professional institutions and the practical needs of policy makers and planners in government and the private sector.

All NPA reports have been authorized for publication in accordance with procedures laid down by the Board of Trustees. Such action does not imply agreement by NPA Board or committee members with all that is contained therein unless such endorsement is specifically stated.

# NPA Officers and Board of Trustees